THE GUILT-FREE GUIDE TO
Your New Life
as a Mom

Practical ways to
take care of yourself,
your life & your baby
—all at the same time

SHERYL GURRENTZ

Illustrated by Ann M. Pickard

PERSPECTIVE
PUBLISHING

LOS ANGELES

Published by Perspective Publishing, Inc.
2528 Sleepy Hollow Dr. #A, Glendale, CA 91206
800-330-5851; 818-502-1270; fax: 818-502-1272;
books@familyhelp.com
www.familyhelp.com

Additional copies of this book may be ordered by calling toll free
1-800-330-5851, or by sending $18.95 ($14.95 + $4 shipping) to the above
address. CA residents add 8% ($1.20) sales tax. Discounts available for quantity
orders. Bookstores, please call LPC Group at 1-800-626-4330.

Library of Congress Cataloging-in-Publication Data

Gurrentz, Sheryl, 1965–
    The guilt-free guide to your new life as a mom : practical ways to take care
of yourself, your life & your baby—all at the same time / Sheryl Gurrentz.—
1st ed.
        p. cm.
    Includes bibliographical references and index.
    ISBN 1-930085-01-X
    1. Motherhood. 2. Mothers. 3. Infants—Care I. Title: your new life as a
mom. II. Title.

HQ759 .G89 2000
306.874′3—dc21

                                                                    00-45653

Illustrations by Ann M. Pickard
Printed in the United States
First Edition

This book is dedicated to:
Monique—who is always a few stages ahead of me
Bridgett—who shared the wonders and frustrations of the
first year of motherhood with me
Cindy, Heidi & Sherri—who let me scrutinize their first
years with their new babies and who are
always there for me and my kids

Acknowledgements

My thanks go to many, many mothers who knowingly or unknowingly shared experiences and ideas that are reflected in this book. I am especially grateful for the contributions of Cindy Ustun, Heidi Dudley, Sherri Kononov, Bridgett Blackburn, Ellen Peterson, Sallie Cohen, Chris Feil, Lori Goldstein, Nicole Gerber, Sherri Goldstein, Monique Weeks, Claudia Miller, Denise O'Connell, Maria Spain, Kay Prince, Wendi Vogt and my own mom, Judith Park. My appreciation also goes to the following people who helped me research, edit and publish this book: Linda Goodman Pillsbury, Stefanie Krasnow, Carol Singer, Robert Beck, Jennifer Bouman, Dr. Raymond Rademacher and the staff of Southeast Denver Pediatrics, Dr. Donald Aptekar, Dr. Nancy McKenzie and the staff of Arapahoe Park Pediatrics, and Jon Tandler. Thanks also to Sharon Cooper, whose comment, "You should write a book!" started the whole process. Finally, my everlasting love and gratitude to my husband Andy, who made me a mom and knows I can't be happy doing just one thing at a time, and to Jordan and Joey, my precious boys who let me practice on them.

Table of Contents

Introduction

I remember crying late one night (early one morning?) as I nursed my first son, two month-old Jordan. I loved my baby, but I was frustrated because every minute of every day seemed exactly the same. I couldn't see the point of trying to go back to sleep or thinking about doing anything but baby care. I felt horrible for not being satisfied with what I was doing, but it seemed like my whole life had been completely replaced with my new responsibilities as a mother. As important as my baby was to me, baby care alone just wasn't enough to make me feel productive and fulfilled.

Luckily, I was loud enough to wake my husband, Andy. He listened to my sob story, then said, "well, why don't you start doing the things you used to do?" His comment was like a bolt of lightning. It hadn't even occurred to me that I was so frustrated because I had lost my sense of self. I had thought that I just needed to work harder at being a good mom and learn to accept the new situation in order to feel better.

Now I realized that I had to learn to be myself and a mother at the same time. As a research-oriented management consultant, I decided that the first step was to find out how other mothers were feeling about it. Since I am also a volunteer birth coach, I talked with my clients about their experiences. I also discussed the issue with many other new moms. I found out that I wasn't alone in wanting to have personal satisfaction and life balance while I was being a terrific mom.

Unfortunately, I also found that there haven't been any resources to help women figure out how to accomplish that goal. Baby books and doctors focus on the baby's development and a woman's physical recovery, but not how she feels about herself and her new lifestyle. Other new moms tend to share what they've done well, such as getting their babies to sleep through the night, and what they enjoy about having a baby. Who wants to admit they've wished they had waited longer to have a baby or hoped that the baby would just go away for a little while?

Your own mother probably won't be able to give you advice about these types of thoughts, either. She can help you learn how to care for a baby, but she may not understand your need for personal satisfaction or be familiar with the lifestyle options you're considering. It's certainly not ideal to look to previous generations of mothers as role models. The baby boomer "supermoms" wanted it all—but found that the pressures of their lifestyles and the stress of trying to get it all left them feeling exhausted. On the other hand, traditional homemakers tended to be involved only in their families and homes and activities that had to do with one or the other. They just weren't expected to have any outside interests. They were supposed to be satisfied if their husbands, homes and children were well cared for.

We are the first generation of mothers to want the best of both worlds, whether or not we work. We want to be able to take care of our own needs and pursue our personal interests in a wide variety of activities inside and outside the home—while we're being great moms. We believe we can balance our personal, professional and parental roles, have an individual identity outside of motherhood and work, and continue our relationships with our partners as adults, not just parents. We are willing to create new, customized lifestyles and career plans that help us achieve our goals. We understand that we can't really have it all—we have to make choices and prioritize what's most important for us, our babies and our families.

Although it is important to acknowledge that you have these expectations, that's not enough. Just knowing what you want doesn't mean it will come to you automatically after your hormones have leveled out or once you've gotten more comfortable taking care of your baby. You have to make it happen. You have to pro-actively go about creating your own personalized version of successful motherhood. It's hard to do that, though, when you don't even know what all your choices are, let alone how they'll affect your life.

That's where this book comes in. It focuses on you and what you'll be thinking about and doing during the first year of motherhood. It realistically defines how life with a baby affects your emotions, your body, your responsibilities and your activities. It also provides a variety of options for avoiding and addressing the concerns that often arise as a result of these changes. My goal as a management and career consultant, birth coach (doula) and fellow mother is to help you create a balanced lifestyle that meets your unique needs and preferences as well as your baby's.

In addition to helping you integrate motherhood into your life without giving up what's important to you, the suggestions will help you do everything you have to do more easily and effectively. By eliminating a lot of trial and error, you'll minimize the amount of mental and physical effort you'll use as you prepare for your activities, juggle the logistics of all your responsibilities and handle the repetitive aspects of baby care. A lot of frustration, and maybe even a bit of resentment about your new role, will be avoided.

You'll end up with more time and energy to play with your baby, enjoy yourself, and be involved in the most important things in your life. You'll be happier and more satisfied overall. This positive attitude will help you be a great mother and a self-confident, capable and productive woman in all the aspects of your life.

Adjusting To Motherhood

Motherhood has many wonderful and rewarding moments, but I'll bet it doesn't turn out to be exactly like you imagined it would be. Sure, when you're pregnant you know intellectually that you're going to be exhausted, overweight and busy around the clock, but there's no way to predict exactly how that will make you feel emotionally. Then, when you're actually a mother, it's easy to think you're not doing a good job if you're not happy and fulfilled all the time. After all, no one wants to feel overwhelmed, frustrated and out of control during such a special time in her life.

The good news is that while few new moms will admit to having them, these types of feelings are not only common—they are completely normal. Moments of joy and wonder do happen, but so do times when you wish the baby would just go away or grow up instantly so you could finally get some sleep. You may feel thrilled, satisfied and joyous one day and trapped, lonely and confused the next.

Instead of trying to ignore your negative feelings, I encourage you to acknowledge them. Once you've done that, you can start to deal with them. The suggestions in this section can help you with both of these challenges. Just because it's normal to have negative feelings doesn't mean you shouldn't try to replace them with more positive ones.

CHAPTER ONE

Feelings About Becoming a Mother

Anticipating Motherhood

If you want to avoid the disappointment of having the realities of motherhood be far different from your fantasies, make sure that your vision of your new life as a mom is as accurate as possible. It's important to think about the various aspects of your life, not just about the baby. Motherhood, after all, is not like baby-sitting. Yes, you'll be doing a lot of baby care, but it won't be in convenient three-hour time segments when baby care is all you'll be doing. It will be almost constant and will have to be done at the same time you're living the rest of your life.

- For a dose of reality, ask a friend with a newborn if you can hang out with her for a day. Tell her you just want to be with her while she goes about her regular activities. Be aware of how many times she gets interrupted at what she's doing, how often she has to do more than one thing at a time and how long it takes her to do everything. Then try to picture yourself in the same situation. If you're really brave, offer to baby-sit at your house while you have other things to do besides take care of the baby.

- It's natural to think that you'll be exactly the same, just with a baby and without a big belly, once you're a mom. It's okay to think that for now, because there's no way to understand how you'll feel emotionally once the baby's born. Just knowing that your perspectives and priorities will change, though, will help you be less surprised when it happens.

- Once the baby is born, your challenge isn't going to be figuring out how to add baby care responsibilities to your list of things to do. It's going to be figuring out how to take care of yourself, your life and your baby all at once. Now is a great time to get used to the idea that you'll have to integrate motherhood into your life, not just add it on as an extra activity.

- Don't feel guilty if you worry about whether you're going to have any time and energy to take care of anything other than the baby. You're not being selfish for wanting to be able to continue to take care of yourself and have some non-mommy fun. Remember, becoming a mom doesn't mean that you lose the right to be a happy, healthy woman with a personal life of her own.

    I was getting so overwhelmed with taking care of my pregnancy that I started to feel like my body wasn't my own. I decided I needed to get back in the habit of taking care of my body for my own sake, not just my baby's. I decided to do something just for me, like getting a massage or giving myself a facial, at least once a week. I feel much happier. I figure it's a good habit to practice now so I'm more likely to take care of myself once the baby is born. (Emma)

- Think about which aspects of yourself, such as being in great physical shape or keeping up with world events or being organized, that you definitely don't want to change when the baby is born. You can even think about what you're going to do to make sure those things don't change. Life as a mom may not turn out exactly like you had expected, but you're more likely to be able to do what's most important to you if you know what your priorities are.

- Discuss parenting techniques and ideas with your partner to make sure you're on the same wavelength about your hopes and expectations about your role as a mother, his as a father and your joint role as parents. Now is a good time to practice making parenting decisions together.

- The aspects of motherhood that you think will be particularly difficult may not be the same ones that seem so difficult after the baby is born. You may not enjoy all the dirty, messy and time-consuming aspects of baby care, for example, but they will be much easier to handle when it's your own baby.

I've done lots of baby-sitting, so I'm no stranger to baby care. I'm good at it, but I get really nauseous when I change a dirty diaper. As silly as it seems, one of my biggest worries when I was pregnant was that I would gag whenever I changed my own baby's diapers. My friends kept telling me that it doesn't make you as sick when it's your own baby's smells. Thank goodness they were right! (Lauren)

- Are you so ready not to be pregnant any more that you think you'll feel fine as soon as the baby is finally born? Sorry. You'll feel different, but not necessarily better. Instead of having heartburn, an almost constant need to urinate and exhaustion, you'll have a sore bottom or incision, painful breasts and exhaustion. Try to focus on the joy of meeting your baby instead of the joy of ending your pregnancy.

- Your baby isn't going to be a newborn for long. Although this stage deserves a lot of thought and preparation, try to think about life with an older baby, too.

- Remember to enjoy the pleasures of life without a baby. Soon it's going to take lots of planning to be able to go to a movie, lots of preparation to go out to dinner and lots of luck to have uninterrupted sex.

- If you're starting to get worried because of what you've read so far, rest assured. It may be a lot of fun to have pastel-tinted, powder-scented fantasies while you're pregnant, but reality is better in the long run. The more you know about what motherhood is really going to be like, the more easily you'll adjust to your new feelings, experiences and responsibilities once the baby is born. You can also use the suggestions in the rest of this book to help you make important lifestyle choices, anticipate and avoid potential problems, get things done easily and effectively, make time to take care of yourself, and create your personalized version of life balance.

The Birth Experience

Giving birth is your first accomplishment as a mother. It's only natural to feel some intense emotions about it. If you're completely happy with your experience, you'll be proud and cherish the memory forever. You can also skip over some of the tips in this section.

If your real birth experience didn't exactly live up to your hopes and plans, however, it's okay to feel a bit disappointed, embarrassed, regretful or even angry afterwards. Take some time to acknowledge and talk about your feelings with your partner, family, friends or doctor, then let those feelings go. Remember that you spent nine months of pregnancy taking good care of your baby. No matter how you delivered, you were successful in giving birth. Try not to let your feelings about your baby's birth interfere with your feelings for your baby.

- If you want to remember every detail of your birth experience, write it down within the first few post-partum days. You may think that the experience of every "ah-hee ah-hoo" and every push are indelibly written in your memory, but there is a natural amnesiac effect that takes place soon after childbirth. Experienced mothers joke that it must be nature's way of making sure that women keep having babies, even after traumatic birth experiences.

- Go ahead, tell every one of your friends each little detail. Sharing delivery stories is one of the favorite pastimes of almost any woman who is or ever plans to be a mother.

- Remember that even if you feel that your body didn't perform the way you wanted it to during labor and delivery, it accomplished an extraordinary task in carrying a growing fetus for nine months. Regardless of how you delivered, you gave birth. Try to focus on the new life you created rather than the way in which you delivered.

- If you are upset about certain aspects of your birth experience, I suggest you get all the details about what went on from someone else who was there, such as your doula, partner or doctor. As a birth coach, I've found that many women think they're remembering exactly what happened, but they really weren't aware of everything. When they get additional information about the medical reasons for certain interventions, they feel less disappointed and more positive about how they did during labor and delivery.

A few days after Madison was born, I was describing my birth experience to a friend. I told her that my birth plan clearly specified that I wanted an all natural birth. I explained that other than an IV and external monitors, I felt I had a fairly natural labor. Things changed during delivery. After I pushed for half an hour, the doctor suddenly seemed angry and yelled for me to push harder. Suddenly there seemed to be one medical intervention after another. Madison was fine after the doctor essentially pulled her out, but I felt like I had failed at pushing. My husband was amazed at my version of the experience. He told me that the doctor didn't think that I couldn't push the baby out, there just wasn't time to wait since the baby's heart rate had dropped dangerously low. I had completely forgotten that fact, if I was ever even aware of it in the first place! Knowing the whole story helped me feel much more confident about myself. Maybe next time I'll get the all natural experience I want. (Heather)

- Many mothers who gave birth by c-section are happy, or at least comfortable, about the way they delivered. Whether you had a scheduled c-section and totally avoided the difficulties of labor, had a c-section after tortuous hours of labor or were rushed into the operating room to ensure the safety of your baby, there are many reasons to be happy and satisfied with your birth experience. If people wrongly assume that you're upset about it, set them straight.

- Some women who gave birth by c-section are upset about not having had the experience of giving birth vaginally. Of course, you're glad that the option of a c-section was available for your own and your baby's health and safety, but it might not have been part of your ideal birth plan. Just remember that you, not the doctors, gave birth. Having a c-section is not a failure. You successfully had a baby. You might not ever be totally happy about the way you delivered, but you probably won't stay upset about it for long.

- It's hard enough to plan the last few weeks of your pregnancy around an unpredictable delivery date. When you unexpectedly deliver by c-section, you have to put your life on hold even longer. Luckily, healing, just like labor, will come. Just hang on and remind yourself that after nine months of taking care of yourself for your baby's sake, what's a few more weeks to take care of yourself for your own sake. You may even come to appreciate the recovery time as an opportunity to relax and enjoy your new baby with few interruptions from everything else in your life.

Maternal Instincts

With pregnancy and delivery over, your focus will shift from your ability to carry a baby to your ability to take care of one. It may be hard to believe that you're really a mother. Many new moms feel as if they're playing dress-up during the first few weeks after giving birth. It's also common for new mothers to feel totally unqualified to be responsible for a helpless little baby. While they expected to know instinctively what to do, they're surprised to find that not everything comes naturally.

Remember that your baby doesn't have any frame of reference other than the one you give him. Luckily, there's rarely only one way to do something. You can both learn and adjust together. Soon you'll see that what you're doing is helping your baby be happy and healthy. Then you'll feel more confident, in control and at ease.

- Even mothers who feel as if they have absolutely no natural maternal instincts are capable of being terrific mothers. It might seem that it takes more of a conscious effort for you to make baby care decisions than for some others, but that isn't going to stop you from making the right choices. Furthermore, other mothers might be making the same effort to arrive at their decisions and choices, but they aren't talking about it. Don't underestimate yourself.

- At some point, you'll just fall in love with your baby. Don't worry if you didn't bond immediately after delivery. Bonding is a process that takes place during the first few days, weeks and months, not just the first few minutes, after a baby is born.

- If you had been hoping for a baby of one sex, it wouldn't be surprising if you feel somewhat disappointed when the baby turns out to be the other. Many new mothers question their natural instincts when they have these feelings. Shouldn't they be thrilled regardless of the sex? How can they be disappointed in their babies? What they're really disappointed about is the loss of a pleasant fantasy. It's not about the baby at all. Acknowledge your feelings, then focus on new, more realistic ideas about your baby's future. This will help you replace the fantasies you created while you were pregnant. You don't have to give up fantasizing, you just need to do it in the context of the new reality. Very soon you won't be able to imagine having had a different baby.

I always envisioned myself being the mother of girls. I couldn't wait to sew dresses, play dress-up, tie hair ribbons and play with Barbie dolls. When Evan was born, I was thrilled that he was healthy and fell in love with him immediately. Nevertheless, I still mourned the fact that my life as a mother wasn't going to be exactly what I had expected. I was nervous about being the mother of a boy, especially since I only had a sister and had never been around many boys. I'm so glad that Dale, my husband, understood that my feelings were about myself and my role, not the baby. I still occasionally think about how things would be if I had a girl, but I have a lot of fun doing the things Evan is interested in. I wouldn't trade having him for the world. (Bridgett)

- Don't be embarrassed if you have a compulsion to sneak in and check if your baby is still breathing. Many of us have done it!

- Don't feel guilty if you are a relaxed and confident mother who doesn't feel the need to constantly check on the baby. If you know your baby is well-cared for and in a safe place, it's good not to be worrying about him constantly.

- Trust your instincts. You know your baby better than anyone else does. Thank people for their suggestions and do what you think is best.

- If your parents were great role models, you're likely to feel confident about how well you can parent your child. If you don't feel that you were well parented, you might feel anxious about your parenting skills. If this is the case for you, remember that poor parenting skills are behaviors not genetic traits. You can break the cycle. Talk to your partner, your friends, your doctor. Take parenting courses at a hospital or community center. There are also counselors, therapists and books available to help you learn a different parenting style.

- As a mother, your instincts are to take every possible measure to make things as perfect as possible for your baby. However, "if it ain't broke, don't fix it." In mommy terms, that translates to, "if your baby is happy, don't change anything." A change might disrupt her. If your baby is quiet and content, don't offer a pacifier, re-arrange the blanket, adjust the slant of the back of the stroller, open the door to check on her (unless you have a real reason to be worried) or do anything else that might upset things.

- Being a mother takes an enormous amount of mental energy. You have to remember what time the baby last ate, how much he ate and when he'll probably need to eat again. You have to plan where you'll be going with the baby and what you'll need to bring with you. You have to consider when the baby napped, how long he napped and what time he'll probably need to nap again. The list goes on and on. Some of us do this subconsciously, but others have to be a little more aware of all this information. This mental activity, along with all the physical activity, explains why you might feel exhausted. Even on a relatively quiet day, you've actually done a lot.

- So you had a fleeting thought of, "I wish this baby would just go away." Maybe the idea of leaving the baby on someone's doorstep has quickly passed through your mind. As long as these thoughts occur infrequently, they embarrass and concern you, and you hug your baby tighter than ever afterwards, you're just venting some frustration. It happens to the best of us.

- When you have negative feelings, examine them carefully. They probably aren't about the baby at all. They're really about how becoming a mother has affected your expectations of yourself and your life, so don't feel guilty about them.

- If you're having serious, frequent feelings of anger toward your baby that you feel could result in any dangerous action, get help. Talk to your partner, your friends, a therapist, your doctor. Most likely, some professional counseling, some assistance in taking care of the baby or some freedom from motherhood, even if it's only for a little while, will do you some good.

Baby Blues and Post-Partum Depression

Along with the joys and frustrations can come some sadness. You know this should be one of the best times in your life, so why do you feel upset? Rather than feeling bad about how you feel, acknowledge it for what it probably is, a hormonal change with emotional effects. Understanding the cause will help you cope. If the situation is more serious, get help.

- Baby blues are a common result of changing hormones, lack of sleep and the let-down after all the excitement of the birth. You might find yourself crying over commercials (not just the Hallmark tear-jerkers), getting upset over the least little thing and avoiding the news because of all the violence and injustice in the world. Most new mothers feel like this for a day or two within the first couple of weeks after baby's birth. Don't worry, you'll get happy!

- Post-Partum Depression is more serious than baby blues. It involves the true symptoms of depression: lack of appetite, lethargy and emotional numbness. If you feel very unhappy, have an extremely difficult time getting up and out of the house, and don't feel like it's getting any better, talk to your doctor. Post-Partum Depression is generally a result of hormones that didn't balance out properly after you gave birth. This is a medical condition that can be treated. It's not your fault. Get some help so you can get on with enjoying your baby and your life again.

- If you have a history of depression, you might need medication to help you get through this sensitive time. Talk to your doctor before a problem develops.

- Even if you aren't depressed or blue, you might still find that the world suddenly seems like a terribly unfit place to raise a little baby. Stories of babies taken from their mothers, suffering with horrible diseases and starving in foreign countries might both fascinate and horrify you at the same time. Whether you can't stand to hear the news or you're compelled to find out about everything that's going on, just follow your instincts. Neither extreme is wrong.

CHAPTER TWO

Feelings About Being a Mother

Getting Used to Being a Mom

Changes often cause stress, even if they're related to something good like having a baby. When you're a new mother who's stressed out, it's easy to feel like things are never going to get better, that this is the permanent new reality. As much as you love your baby and as happy as you are to have her, you may feel as if everything in your life now revolves around her.

Luckily, babies grow up and mothers adapt. The suggestions in this chapter will help you look at this time as a time of adjustment. It's a phase that you will get through. When you're more used to feeling like a mother, you may still feel some of the same emotions, but they won't make you as stressed.

- Remember how special you felt when you were pregnant? You probably kept on feeling special just after your baby was born—you created that incredible baby. After the initial excitement over the birth wears off, though, you have to adjust to the baby, not you, being the center of attention. It's hard to keep feeling special and important when your tummy bulges, your breasts leak and you can't manage to get showered and dressed until mid-day. When this occurs, remind yourself that you are totally responsible for a tiny person's health and happiness. Motherhood is sometimes a thankless and demanding task, but it's also an incredibly important and fulfilling one.

- Lack of sleep can do strange things. You might feel like you're operating in a fog. You might feel edgy and lack the ability to cope, even when it's just the little things that go wrong. Do for yourself what you'd do for your baby if he was tired—reduce the amount of stimulation around you, decrease your expectations regarding what you can accomplish and try to nap. At first it might be difficult to just lie down in the middle of the day, but try to clear your mind, take the phone off the hook and give yourself permission to be "lazy." Even if you have a hard time falling asleep during the day, take the time to relax while the baby is napping or amusing himself.

- If you like to keep busy, you probably feel most satisfied when you're getting things done. As a new mother, you're going to have to balance your body's need for rest with your mind's need for stimulation and accomplishment. Consciously evaluate which is more important each time you have a break from mommy-related duties.

  My version of relaxing is getting things done. I've never been the type to lie down and rest. I feel better if I've accomplished something. When Caley is napping, I try to do something that makes me feel good. Lots of times I do my nails, read my book club book or get my house organized. As long as I'm not doing something baby-related, I feel more rested afterwards. (Amy)

- Don't be surprised to find that even when you do get time alone, you still think of the baby. It's very common for new mothers to have a hard time getting their minds off their babies. It might take a while before you can unwind and stop feeling like you're forgetting something or should be doing something else. As your baby gets older and you get more used to going out without her, you'll feel more like yourself even though your sense of responsibility will continue to be a full-time reality.

- On the flip side, many new mothers are afraid that they'll forget their babies and leave them in the house, in the car or wherever they are visiting. While it has happened, you aren't likely to go very far before you remember that you're a mother now. It won't take many outings before taking the baby along seems perfectly natural. Then you'll stop worrying about leaving her behind.

Jeff and I used to laugh about a commercial in which busy parents leave the baby in the high chair when they rush out of the house. Then it sort of happened to us. We both thought the other had brought Becca to the car. We joked about it, but we were relieved to realize that there's no way we could have even gotten as far as pulling out of the garage without missing her. (Wendi)

- You might feel like you're looking at the world through "baby-colored" glasses. You perceive everything in terms of how it relates to you as a mother instead of considering things more objectively. This perception, which might have begun during your pregnancy, seems to last for a long time. When you're raising a small child, you do need to consider things in a different manner. You can't just think about yourself. You must also be aware of how your baby is affected. Once again, this is just part of being a mother. You'll get used to it.

My husband and I were designing a new home just after Michael was born. I kept asking the builder to make changes, such as moving the shower knobs and the door locks higher, to toddler-proof the house. He finally said, "Lady, you're not going to have a baby forever." I reminded him that I had years of baby-proofing ahead of me with this baby and any future babies. He stopped making fun of me, but his perspective helped me remember that baby-proofing wasn't going to be an issue forever. (Donna)

- It takes time to develop the skill of simultaneously being aware of what your baby is doing and what's going on around you. At first, you might need to tune everything else out while you focus on your baby. During this time, you might find that other people don't realize, for example, that you can't listen to them or carry on a conversation while you're dealing with the baby. To avoid the frustration of having people talk at you while you're trying to concentrate on something else, ask them to "hold that thought for a moment while I take care of the baby." Soon you'll be in the habit of caring for the baby. You'll be able to do more than one thing at a time again.

It took a long time to figure out why I was becoming so irritated and tense whenever one of my husband's best friends, who was single, joined us for dinner during the first months after Jonathan was born. The problem was that I was feeling left out because the conversation kept going while I was paying attention to the baby. Our friend was frustrated because I seemed to be ignoring him. Luckily, he learned that he needed to take a break from talking when I was concentrating on the baby. I got better at doing two things at once. We also started getting baby-sitters so we could go out and have long, intense conversations. (Dawn)

- Even if everything is going smoothly, but especially when it isn't, you might find yourself feeling sad that motherhood isn't exactly as you had imagined. Acknowledge your sense of loss for that perfect world of your daydreams, but rest assured. Most new mothers find reality to be more deeply fulfilling than the fantasy. At the same time, remember that while being a mother means that you can't be totally in control of your own time and activities, you can still make choices that make your life more enjoyable and fulfilling.

- When you're feeling down or overwhelmed with your baby care responsibilities, I recommend that you do something for yourself. Even something small such taking a long, hot bath yourself instead of bathing the baby, reading a newspaper or novel instead of a baby-related book, or painting your fingernails instead of cleaning the house while the baby naps will help you feel better—as long as you don't let yourself feel guilty.

- When you get the intense feeling that you're going to be changing diapers and feeding a baby forever, talk with parents of school-age kids. They'll reassure you that things will get much easier in the not-to-distant future. Try to believe them even though a few months may seem like a light-year to you at this point. Parents of toddlers and preschoolers can tell you the same thing, but they'll probably also tell you about the difficulties of the stages you'll be facing next. Right now, it's better to focus on large improvements, even if they are a while away, rather than on substituting one challenge for another.

- Lots of new mothers go through periods when they feel frustrated, out of control, angry, resentful and regretful. No, you didn't make a huge mistake by becoming a mother. No, you're no less qualified to be one than the rest of us. Yes, you're going through the normal experiences of motherhood, in the first year and beyond.

On really rough days, my best friend and I know that we can call each other up to say, "Remind me again why we wanted to have babies!" We listen to each other's mother-related troubles, acknowledge each other's feelings and offer recommendations for making things better. We always hang up knowing we'll feel better soon, even if the situation doesn't resolve itself immediately. (Tracey)

• There's nothing wrong with saying (not screaming) something like, "You're driving me crazy today," to your baby. He won't understand, but it might make you feel better. You can't expect to be totally in love and blissfully happy with your baby at all times. You still love him. You just don't love how he's behaving at that point in time.

• Don't feel bad if you fantasize about what life will be like when your baby isn't a baby anymore. You might even fast-forward to when he's off to camp or college. This is a normal way to work off stress. It helps to remember that at some point, things will get easier. Being a mother won't always be such an all-encompassing role.

• Some mothers worry that they'll resent the fact that they now have to go to family-oriented places, give up doing certain things and spend so much time with the baby. What they usually find is that they now want to do family-oriented activities and love spending time with their babies. Once you're a mother, your priorities and preferences change. Just don't get so caught up in kid-related fun that you give up all your adult time.

• Who says that people have to totally grow up once they become parents? Now you have an excuse to make funny noises, sing silly songs and dance around the room, go to amusement parks, play with toys and go to Disney movies. Enjoy it. Being responsible doesn't mean that you have to be boring.

One of my favorite experiences was when Haley outgrew all the newborn toys she'd received as baby gifts. I decided to take her to the toy store to get her some toys that were more advanced. I had a great time looking at all the baby toys that had recently come on the market, but the best part was recognizing toys that I had loved as a child. I felt like I was the kid in the toy store. I actually bought a few games and toys for her to use when she's a lot older because I really wanted to have them for myself. I can't wait to play with them with her. (Cori)

It's been years since I gave myself the time and permission to really play and act child-like. With Neal, I find myself down on the floor, rolling around, laughing and being totally silly. It's such a joy to share this kind of time with him. (Jennifer)

- Even in the midst of all the frustrations of motherhood you'll have many moments of pure pleasure. Sometimes in the strangest of places, you'll just break out in a huge smile when you suddenly remember, "hey, this is my baby and I'm a mommy!" Enjoy the sensation. Try to remember it when things are more difficult.

Handling Your Feelings About Your Baby's Changes

While you're getting used to being a mother, your baby is growing and changing, too. It's natural for you to feel more "in love" with your baby during some stages and more frustrated in others. The good news is that babies grow and change so quickly that your baby will rapidly progress through particularly difficult stages. The bad news is that he'll also rapidly progress through any stage that you particularly love.

- Be sure to take the time to savor each stage in your baby's development. You don't want to feel that you didn't fully appreciate each opportunity to create a special memory. Right now, for example, it might feel as if you'll be nursing or rocking a baby forever. In reality, though, as soon as your baby is active and mobile, it will be hard to remember exactly what it felt like when she was totally relaxed and calm in your arms.

- One of the hardest parts about being in a difficult stage is that you don't know how long it will last, so you can't anticipate the light at the end of the tunnel. It can be helpful to talk to moms whose babies are a few months older to find out about their babies' timelines. They'll confirm that certain stages seem endless while you're going through them even though they really don't last that long. You may not believe them, but I promise it's true.

When Bonnie was first eating solid food, I felt like I was going to be sitting in front of a high chair for the rest of my life. When Ethan came along, I looked back at Bonnie's baby book and realized that I only spoon-fed her for three months before she fed herself. This stage seemed a lot shorter and more enjoyable the second time around. (Alicia)

- Baby books offer helpful information on when to expect different stages and how long those stages are likely to last. Just don't get hung up on the exact timelines they provide. Your baby may progress at a very different pace.

- A baby book or diary is a wonderful way to acknowledge your feelings about your baby's personality and development. When you're feeling sentimental, it can be very comforting to read a written account of your baby's history.

- Be sure to date photos and videos. Right now you think you'll remember everything. After some time passes, especially if you have another baby, the memories of when things happened may get somewhat fuzzy.

- If you're too busy or not the type to keep a baby album, a baby box is an easy alternative. Start a new box each year, then just put your mementos and pictures in whenever you can.

- If you're usually the photographer, make an effort to have someone else take pictures occasionally so there are some pictures of you with your baby, too.

- As your baby nears his first birthday, it's both an exciting and a melancholy time. It's hard to believe that it's been a whole year. If you feel that that your baby is turning into a toddler, spend some time with a two year-old to reassure yourself that your child is still fairly baby-like. Think back and remember how far you and your baby have come in the past year. Praise yourself for doing such a good job raising your baby and for overcoming the many challenges of the past year.

Section Two

Creating Life Balance

Even though you were used to thinking about your own needs and interests before you became a mother, I'll almost guarantee you that it won't feel natural after you give birth. Your instinct as a new mother is to focus almost exclusively on the baby. You won't plan on neglecting your own needs, of course. I'm sure you intend to handle all the other stuff in your life. You'll get around to it when you can!

Unfortunately, when you're a mom, times "when you can" will be rare. Baby care will fill up all your time if you let it. What's more, motherhood has a funny way of changing your priorities and preferences about almost everything you want and need to do. Doing a great job of being a mom becomes so important that you feel torn. Part of you feels that nothing is as important as your mommy-related responsibilities. You tend to put those things first, even if you'd like to be doing some activities that aren't related to the baby. If you're not careful, you could easily get into the habit of always putting yourself last on the list.

If you want to be a great mom, feel satisfied as a mother and a person, and balance motherhood with everything else you want to do, you must make a conscious effort to take care of your own needs and preferences while you're taking care of your baby. To do this, you have to examine your new priorities, plan for activities that are relaxing and satisfying to you, and be realistic about what can and can't be accomplished.

Motherhood should be a wonderful, important part of you, but not all of you. You should have the time and energy for other parts of your life, too. Unless you create that time and energy, though, you probably won't get it.

CHAPTER THREE

Getting Things Done

Managing During the First Weeks at Home

Most new mothers plan to spend at least a few weeks at home, primarily taking care of the baby and recuperating. Expectations for this period, whether or not it's a formal maternity leave, tend to run high. It's important to give yourself permission to take it easy and enjoy this short break so you can create realistic, achievable expectations for now and the future. Then you'll be able to transition back into the rest of your life more easily when this special phase of motherhood is over.

- Clearly communicate your desires and expectations to people helping you during the first few days or weeks at home. Do you want help with the housework so you can concentrate on the baby? If so, what housework would you like them to do? How would you like them to do it? Do you prefer to have someone diaper, dress and check on the baby so you can rest and recuperate? Or do you prefer to have someone with you while you care for the baby? If they want to assist you, they most likely won't mind some suggestions on how they can be most helpful. It won't do anyone any good to criticize or resent their efforts after the fact.

- A common frustration of new moms is that time during the first six weeks of motherhood seems to slow to a crawl. Now this may seem like a good thing if you only have six weeks of maternity leave and you want to drag it out, but it can get frustrating when it seems like changing diapers, doing laundry and feeding the baby are the only things you're doing—and you're going to be doing them around the clock forever. The reason new moms feel this way is that life is now taking place in increments of two or three hours instead of four or eight hours. That can make each day feel like several. Six weeks can feel like six months. Don't worry. As your baby starts lengthening the time in between feedings as well as the time she sleeps at night, your perception of time will return to normal.

- Did you used to wonder what people who were home with a baby did all day long? Now that you have six weeks or so, do you think that you're going to read all the best-selling novels, organize all your closets, thoroughly clean your house, plant flowers, train the dog and purge your files? Think again. During those first few weeks, your days are anything but free time. Sure, the baby sleeps a lot, but you also need extra naps to recover from nighttime feedings. Yes, the only other thing that the baby does is eat, but that can take up to an hour per session. Furthermore, an unpredictable schedule that revolves around three hour time segments doesn't leave you with much energy to accomplish miracles. Be realistic about how much of your "to do" list you can complete.

> Back when I was working and hadn't had a baby yet, I was somewhat judgmental about friends who were staying home with their babies, yet complaining that they were so busy with baby care that they couldn't get anything else done. There seemed to be so much time during the day that I just couldn't understand it—until I had Ryan, that is! Then I realized that it is easy to get everything done when you can be scheduled and organized. When you're at the baby's beck and call, it's a lot different. (Stefanie)

- It may not be enough to just reduce the number of things you want to get done in a certain day or week. You might also need to adjust your expectations about the pace you can maintain while you do them. You're giving a lot of time and attention to your baby, he causes lots of interruptions and you're exhausted. As a result, each activity might take longer than it used to. Patience with yourself is definitely a virtue.

- If you find yourself obsessed with how often your baby is eating, how long it takes her to eat, how much she's sleeping and how many times you wake up in the middle of the night, I recommend that you live without a clock for a few days or weeks. It doesn't really matter what time it is. When the baby is hungry you feed her, when she's wet you change her and when she needs to sleep, she will. It's more important that you pay attention to the signals she's giving you than to what the clock says.

- If you plan on going back to work, continue to use your appointment book, even if you're just scheduling lunch with a friend. Call your boss, co-workers and clients to tell them about your baby. Call in to work occasionally to find out what's going on. Just don't get too involved— you're at home for a good reason.

- Many mothers who previously couldn't imagine wanting to stay at home with their babies are shocked when they find the thought of returning to work horrifying. If at all possible, don't lock yourself into anything right now. Explore your options. Maybe your employer will be willing to discuss flex time, part-time or a home office as options. An extended maternity leave is another option. Other career strategies are described in Section Seven.

- Many new moms look forward to returning to work and resuming their non-mommy activities. These feelings aren't anything to feel guilty about, either. Make sure to fully appreciate your maternity leave, make appropriate plans to handle the logistics of going to work and enjoy the variety of pleasures in your life.

Balancing Your Responsibilities

It's very hard to predict what you will and won't do when you're a mother until you actually are one. If you made "I would never . . ." or "I will always . . ." statements when you were pregnant, you may have to eat your words now that you realize how much motherhood affects what you want to do, what you can do, how much you do and how well you can do it. As important as your personal activities, plants and pets are, for example, the baby becomes the number one priority—as it should be.

The challenge becomes one of managing all your responsibilities and interests to make sure that each gets the time and attention it deserves.

Many of the tasks that need to be performed, such as feeding and diapering, aren't optional. There are choices about who will do them and how they're going to get done, but not whether or not to do them at all. So, you have to continually make choices about the relative importance of everything else.

- Before you had a baby, you probably found that if you couldn't get something done immediately, you could find time to do it later. Now you might find that if you don't get something done when you planned on doing it, it never gets done. To help minimize the feeling that you're always running behind, give yourself longer deadlines. Instead of planning on doing something today, for example, make your goal to get it done this week.

- You are not the only one who became a parent. Just because a certain responsibility used to be yours doesn't necessarily mean that it should continue to be yours. Every so often, you and your partner should reassign the responsibilities involved in running a home, caring for a baby, working and doing everything else that needs to get done.

    I used to take the laundry to the dry cleaner because it was on my way to work. Once Kevin was born, though, it was really difficult to carry him and the laundry at the same time. At first my husband resisted taking over this responsibility because the dry cleaner was out of the way for him. After wasting a few minutes trying to figure out how and when he could get there, we realized there was an easier way. We could just find a new dry cleaner that was on his way to work! (Chloe)

- Many new mothers experience forgetfulness. In reality, it's not that you're forgetting more than you used to, it's just that you have so much more to remember and think about. The non-mommy-related details of your life may be overlooked. Try making lists. Just be sure to write things down as soon as you think of them (otherwise, you may forget!) and put your lists in places where they can easily be seen so you won't get too busy to look at them.

    I found that it helped me keep track of my "to-do" list if I kept pads of sticky notes all over the house and in the car. Whenever I thought of something important, I jotted it down. I put notes for things that had to be done outside the house onto Ari's diaper bag. Notes about things at home got posted on the refrigerator. I couldn't help but see them. (Becky)

- As you complete the items on your "to-do" list, check them off or cross them out. Not only will this help you see what's left to do, but it will help you see tangible evidence that you really have accomplished something.

- Adding a baby to your life is a wonderful, but complicated process. Sometimes you have to recognize that it's not enough to try to find the time and energy to do everything. You also have to realize that maybe you can't do everything. Often the best solution to the dilemma of how to juggle all your responsibilities is to eliminate some of them. Wait a few weeks or months, until you've settled into a comfortable pattern of motherhood, then focus on your life as a whole. What continues to be important to you? What no longer matters as much? Be willing to change how you handle the non-mommy aspects of your life so you can eliminate some stress and get more enjoyment out of everything you do.

- In addition to eliminating some of your "to do" items, you may also have to change how you do the things you keep on your list. Evaluate the various aspects of your life, including everything from your volunteer duties to the way you clean house to how you get your errands done. What can someone else do? What can be done less intensely or more efficiently?

- Try not to get so busy with all the responsibilities that have to be handled that you forget to relax and have fun. If necessary, schedule regular times in your day or week to sit down and play with your baby, have fun with your friends, spend special time with your partner and enjoy time by yourself.

- Committing to do things or meet people at a specific time can cause a lot of frustration. Instead, I suggest you commit to a certain period of time, such as between 12:00 and 12:30 (instead of at 12:15). That way, you can still make the target time even if the baby has a dirty diaper or needs to nurse just as you're about to walk out the door.

- Even if your pet used to be your pride and joy, your "baby," you might find that it's getting much less attention from you than it used to. Don't feel bad that your pet has moved down on your list of priorities. Just make sure to take care of its basic needs and give it some attention. Also remember that your baby will soon be old enough to give the pet some additional attention and interaction.

- Don't be surprised to find that your plants occasionally get a bit wilted. With everything else you're doing, watering plants is something that's easy to put off until you have more time. That isn't in your plants' best interests, of course, but at least they aren't screaming to be fed. You might even want to consider silk plants instead of real ones.

- Don't feel guilty if your house-cleaning standards aren't as high as they used to be. Housework is a responsibility that often gets neglected when there's a baby in the house. Prioritize which aspects of house cleaning are the most important to you.

- If your expectations about the cleanliness of your house remain high, that's fine. Just be sure you and your partner adjust your schedules so you'll have time to take care yourselves as well as your baby and your house. Either plan a regular time to clean, make an effort to clean one or two areas a day or consider hiring someone else to help on a permanent or short-term basis.

> *Before I had a baby, I swore that I'd never let my house get as messy as some I had seen. My husband even made me promise that our house would never be covered with toys. Having a clean and neat house had always been extremely important to both of us. Since Caitlyn was born, though, we've had to redefine our concept of "neat and clean." When it comes down to cleaning the house or being with the baby, Caitlyn wins. The surprising thing is that the added mess in the house doesn't seem to bother us as much as we had thought it would. (Julie)*

- If work is one of the responsibilities you need to juggle, please see Chapter 21. This topic deserves a whole chapter of its own.

CHAPTER FOUR

Making Time for Yourself

Just because you have someone else to take care of doesn't mean you should stop taking care of yourself. It's important that you continue to participate in adult activities, get together with friends and do things that help you maintain your sense of personal identity. Being a mom doesn't mean that you should give up who you are and what's important to you. It does mean that sometimes you have to try a little harder to get your own needs met.

- Declare at least a few minutes each day as your private, non-mommy time. Some mothers like to take their break at the same time every day. Others like to take it when they need it. It's good for your baby to learn to be by himself for a little while and, as he gets older, to understand that mommy is a person, too, and needs time to do adult things. Besides, you'll feel more in control, more relaxed and more sane if you have time to do what you want when you want—even if you only have those choices during a fifteen minute period. As your baby gets older you might be able to make this alone time longer and longer. Of course, be sure that he's is in a safe place when he's left unsupervised.

  The time when I shower and dress has always been the time when I like to be alone to think about everything I have to do that day, daydream and just relax. When Alec was born, I decided that my habit didn't have to change. He's now four and he knows to respect my time in the morning. (Susan)

- There's nothing wrong if you don't want take a shower, style your hair, put on make-up or get dressed on a daily basis. If you want to do some or all of these things, however, don't let having a baby stop you. If your baby is fed, changed and in a safe place with something interesting to look at or listen to, it won't hurt her to be without you for a little while —even if she fusses.

> *At first, finding time to get showered and dressed was next to impossible. After a few weeks, though, I was tired of spending the day in my nightgown. So I gave myself a goal to work toward. At first, I tried to be dressed by noon. Then, I tried to be dressed by eleven o'clock. After a while, I adjusted my goal back to ten o'clock, then to nine o'clock. Giving myself a realistic, achievable goal made me feel good about accomplishing something for myself on those crazy mornings.* (Vivian)

> *I know I deserve some time to take care of myself, but I still feel guilty about it. It helps to think of the safety instructions on airplanes: put your own oxygen mask on first, then take care of others who need assistance. It reminds me that I can't do a good job of taking care of Colleen if I'm not okay myself.* (Ginger)

- If you're nervous about leaving your baby alone while you shower and dress, bring him into the bathroom with you. Or, take your shower when he's napping. Do what it takes to create a relaxing time for taking care of yourself.

- Create a place in your home that is yours and yours alone. Baby paraphernalia and your partner's mail are not allowed. With baby stuff taking over your house and a schedule that is constantly changing, it will probably be nice to have one place that doesn't change unless you change it. Even if it's a closet or a small kitchen desk instead of a lovely room, it will be someplace that is totally under your control.

- Everyone needs time alone—some need more, some less. If you're staying home with the baby, it can be difficult to watch your partner's seeming ability to come and go as he pleases without thinking about the baby. You might feel so tied down to the baby that you're actually jealous when your partner leaves for work. Going to the dentist might even start sounding like a fun thing to do, as long as you can go alone. Have your partner watch the baby, hire a baby-sitter, ask grandma to come over, or do whatever it takes to get some time to yourself. Even if all you do is go to the grocery store for an hour between feedings, you'll feel much better.

- Use nursing or bottle-feeding sessions as opportunities to totally relax. Sometimes you can do nothing but enjoy touching and looking at your baby. Sometimes you can read a book, watch TV or talk on the phone while you feed him. Don't try to accomplish anything during these special times. These may be the only chances to relax you get for a while.

> When Craig and I settled into a comfortable, easy nursing pattern, I thought I could start getting things done while I nursed. I quickly found that it was hard to carry on important phone conversations while I was moving him from one breast to the other. I couldn't hold papers while I was burping him. I also learned that he didn't nurse as well because I was getting tense. Now I just read a novel or call friends if I feel like doing something while I nurse. (Lydia)

- Stay involved with activities that satisfy your personal needs and interests. You might find that you want to scale back the level of commitment you can offer, but you shouldn't look at it as an all-or-nothing situation. Most organizations will be happy to let you take it easy for a while. Many hobbies can be done less frequently or intensely. It's good to maintain some level of involvement so it's easier to resume more activity when you're ready. If you do decide to take a complete break, I suggest you give yourself a specific time frame, including a date when you'll re-evaluate your decision.

- You may have heard other new mothers complain that they're desperate for adult conversation, preferably some that doesn't involve the baby. To avoid that frustration, encourage your partner to share his day with you, discuss current events and plan events for you as a couple. Talk with people everywhere you go. Sign up for a class or discussion group. Don't let your baby be the only person you talk to.

- Keep in touch with your friends, even if it's only through occasional phone calls or e-mail. While you might find that you tend to develop strong relationships with other new mothers, losing old friends can make you feel as if you're losing part of your past. It's also nice to talk with people who know you as more than just your child's mother. Talking about the topics that interest your childless friends will also help you have some adult conversations that don't revolve around babies.

- It's great when you can meet other new moms while you pursue your personal interests. You can enroll in a post-natal exercise class or a mom and tot play group. These are sponsored by recreation centers, athletic clubs, religious organizations, and community colleges. You can join or create a book group with other moms. Another idea is to take a walk to a playground so your baby can nap in the sun while you do some reading or chat with other moms.

- Initiate conversations with new mothers wherever you go. Admire a baby or comment on something you have in common and you'll be talking before you know it. You'll probably find that other new moms will also welcome the opportunity to create a connection with women in a similar stage of life.

- Don't be afraid to discuss your concerns and frustrations with other new moms. Chances are what you're experiencing isn't uncommon. Other new mothers can help you gain perspective, vent emotion and discover other ways to deal with the situations you face.

> *I reluctantly joined a playgroup with my friend. I didn't really want to go because I felt like I was thinking and talking about my baby enough. Instead, I wanted to be involved with women who weren't talking about their babies. After talking with other new moms, though, I realized that sharing our thoughts on motherhood made me feel more in control. We were talking like intelligent people about how to solve our problems, make our lives easier and have more fun with our babies. We weren't comparing house cleaning tips or sharing recipes. I liked helping other women figure out how to handle their situations and having them help me brainstorm about mine. I still like going to professional meetings, but playgroup is really important to me, too.* (Ruth)

- The Internet is a great resource. Not only does it have lots of websites that provide information specifically for new moms, but the chat rooms are a great way to "talk" to someone when you can't get out of the house. Don't forget that you can look up and chat about non-mommy-related stuff, too!

Dealing With Physical Changes

After nine months of pregnancy, I'm sure you're ready to call your body your own and return to normal. The truth is, you probably won't feel "normal" for a while, especially if you're nursing. Even then, your new normal may turn out to be somewhat different from your old normal.

While most of the physical effects of giving birth will probably disappear during the six-week post-partum period, your body has gone through a lot. The changes it experienced during the nine months of pregnancy take longer to go away. If you ignore your body's needs, you'll only make the physical recovery longer and more difficult. Your body deserves time and attention during the weeks and months after your baby's birth so it can create the new normal as quickly and comfortably as possible.

I know this is easier said than done while you're learning to take care of your baby. It's easy to put off washing your face before you collapse into bed, forgo the makeup in the morning, or concede defeat over your exercise routine. Trust me, though. It's worth the effort to take care of yourself. You'll be better able to cope with exhaustion, not to mention carrying all that baby stuff, if you're healthy. It will be more appealing to get out of the house or be involved with non-mommy activities if you're happy about how you look and feel. You'll have more fun playing with your baby if you're comfortable. You'll enjoy sex more if you and your partner are aware of what feels good to you now that you've given birth and are caring for a baby.

CHAPTER FIVE

The First Days After Childbirth

After a Vaginal Delivery

Regardless of the length or intensity of your labor and delivery, you've just been through a major physical ordeal. You should give yourself the time and permission to recuperate and take it easy—whether or not you feel particularly sore and tired in the first few weeks after delivery. Taking care of yourself helps speed recovery, making it easier to care for your baby and resume your normal activities.

- You probably expect to have some discomfort between your legs during the first few days after a vaginal delivery. If you had a difficult delivery, particularly if you had a long pushing stage, there are likely to be some other after-effects of childbirth, too. You might have broken blood vessels in your face, giving you a bruised look. You might have a backache and sore muscles. You may experience urinary incontinence. Your eyes could be bloodshot. Your shoulders might even hurt. These are common discomforts that should gradually disappear. If they aren't going away as quickly as you think they should, talk with your doctor.

    I always say that I had "butt labor," not back labor. (Cindy)

- Your perineum (the area between your vagina and rectum) may be sore even if you didn't have an episiotomy. It was stretched a lot—just look at the size of your baby's head!

What to Try: To Make Your Vaginal or Perineal Area More Comfortable

PUSH YOUR BUTTOCKS TOGETHER as you lower yourself to sit down.

WHEN YOU GO FROM SITTING TO STANDING, LIFT YOURSELF STRAIGHT UP, without sliding along the chair or bed.

SIT ON FIRM SURFACES instead of soft ones in which you'd sink down.

SIT ON AN INVALID RING, an inflatable, donut-shaped pillow. If you don't have one, ask for one from the hospital to make the ride home more comfortable.

PAT, INSTEAD OF WIPE, WITH TOILET PAPER. Or, squirt water to clean yourself instead of using toilet paper.

SQUAT OVER THE TOILET AND TILT YOUR HIPS so that urine doesn't flow over the sore spot.

TUCK A HEMORRHOID PAD OVER THE STITCHES, leaving it there until you change your pad the next time or until you're uncomfortable and need additional relief.

APPLY AN ANESTHETIC HEMORRHOID CREAM or other cream recommended by your doctor on the sore area.

PUT THE ANESTHETIC HEMORRHOID CREAM ON A HEMORRHOID PAD and use both methods at the same time.

USE A BAG OF FROZEN PEAS wrapped in a washcloth as an ice pack.

SOAK IN A WARM BATH two to four times a day. If you're extremely sore, sit on an inflatable doughnut pillow and make sure to have help getting in and out of the tub during the first few days.

WEAR CLOTHING THAT FITS LOOSELY in the crotch.

- The thought of having your first bowel movement after childbirth is dreadful. It's frightening to think that if you push too hard you'll rip your stitches. Fortunately, the chances of that happening are very small. Even if you don't have stitches, maybe you're just so sore that any effort at all is painful. Try to relax about the whole thing. You probably won't have to deal with it for at least a couple of days. Take a stool softener (not a laxative) if your doctor okays it, drink fluids and, most importantly, go when the urge strikes. It might hurt, but it won't be nearly as bad as what you went through during childbirth. You can take it.

- Be extremely careful not to get any fecal material onto the site of an episiotomy or vaginal tear. Wipe front to back.

- Bladder problems after delivery aren't uncommon. Signs of a bladder infection include frequent urination in small amounts, a burning sensation when you urinate that seems to be internal, not external (not at the site of an episiotomy or perineal tear), an intense urge to urinate (even if you just went) and a fever of over 100.4 degrees. Consult with your doctor if you think you might have a bladder infection.

- Pushing a baby out takes a toll on the vagina. Your vagina might not feel as "tight" for a while. Another common change, especially after second, third or additional deliveries, is the sensation that something is sagging down into your vagina. This might be a condition called uterine prolapse, when the uterus actually does drop down a little. You might find the problem becomes worse when you cough or strain on the toilet. In most cases, the muscle tone will return and the uncomfortable sensation will subside when your period returns and your estrogen production is back to normal. It might be helpful to do Kegel exercises (contract then release the vaginal muscles as you would to stop and start a stream of urine). If the condition is really bothering you, talk to your doctor.

- Another common problem related to lax muscles is urine that leaks when you cough or sneeze. Kegels and time should help this condition, too.

After a Cesarean Delivery

Everyone knows that women who deliver by c-section tend to have more difficult recoveries than those who delivered vaginally. Even so, many new mothers who had c-sections don't give their bodies enough credit. Remember that you not only have to experience the physical changes that accompany giving birth, but also the after-effects of abdominal surgery. If you went through labor and pushing, you may even have some of the previously described symptoms associated with a vaginal birth.

- The sooner you get up and move around, the better. Walking helps move around any gas that got trapped in your body during the surgery.

While you'll probably feel like hunching over and protecting those sore abdominal muscles, it's better to straighten up.

- Passing gas is a very good sign after a c-section, since it indicates that your internal organs are beginning to regain their normal function. Forget about being ladylike. When you need to pass gas, do it—no matter who is there or where you are. As I like to remind new moms, after all the indignities involved in labor and delivery, what's a little gas! Any sense of modesty should be long gone.

- When you're in pain, it can be difficult to rest, relax and interact with your baby. Don't be afraid to take pain medication. There are a variety of drugs which won't affect your milk or your ability to care for yourself and your baby.

- If you want pain medication but haven't been offered any, ask for some. Doctors sometimes instruct nurses to give pain medication upon request. Unless you ask, you won't get it.

- Don't be afraid of having your stitches or staples removed. Most women find that it's virtually painless.

- Carefully choose the outfit to wear when you leave the hospital. High-waisted underpants and a loose jumper are safe choices. You don't want anything that could rub on the incision.

- If you're going to drive away from the hospital in a vehicle which is higher than a traditional car, have the person picking you up bring a sturdy stool. Trying to climb up into a high vehicle without one can be very difficult.

- You should contact your doctor if you have any of the following symptoms:

  ❑ Fever of over 100.4 degrees

  ❑ Increased tenderness, swelling, heat or redness around the scar or skin near the scar

  ❑ Discharge from the incision

❏ Foul-smelling vaginal discharge

❏ Pain in your uterus

- During the first week after giving birth, you can expect almost every movement to be somewhat uncomfortable. It might be particularly difficult to turn over in bed, climb stairs and go from sitting to standing. You'll probably require prescription pain medication fairly regularly. Take everything slowly and easily!

- Place a high-backed chair next to the bed and toilet. Use the back of the chair to lean on as you sit down and get up.

- Make sure that you have a drink, a snack, the baby, diapers, diaper wipes, a container for the dirty diapers, the phone, the remote control, a book or whatever else you might need within reach when you get situated in a particular spot. There's nothing worse than gingerly moving from the bed to the couch, only to have the phone ring across the room two minutes later.

- There's nothing wrong with spending the first few days at home in bed. There's no reason to do anything else unless you want to.

  I loved being in bed for a few days after I got home from the hospital. I kept Talia right next to me and did nothing else but take care of her, rest, read and watch TV. After many uncomfortable nights in the last month and a long and difficult labor, I appreciated the chance to rest and relax. (Andrea)

- Whether you like it or not, you're going to need some help during the first few weeks. If you don't have, or don't want, a family member or friend to help you, you can get hired help to provide baby care assistance until you're stronger. Look for advertisements for baby doulas or baby nurses in local parenting magazines. You can also look in the yellow pages under "nanny" to find services that provide short-term, part-time help. A cleaning service can come for a few weeks to take care of your house. Driving services, taxis or buses are options for getting around before you can drive.

- Be honest with your family and friends about the help you need. If you give yourself the recovery time you need at the beginning, you might reduce the recovery time you need overall. When people offer to help you with cleaning, cooking, laundry or baby care, take them up on it.

- Don't do too much the first day that you feel significant improvement. If you do, you're likely to find yourself back in bed again the next day. Gently and gradually increase your activity level.

- Don't do more when you're taking pain medication than you would do when you're not. The medication masks pain, which is a good indicator of whether or not you should be doing something.

- You don't need to answer the phone every time it rings. An answering machine or service can be a wonderful thing. Don't be afraid to use it. You can even turn the ringer off when you are trying to rest. Return calls when you're ready. People will understand.

More After-Effects of Childbirth

In addition to the physical experiences that relate directly to how you delivered, there are a few more that almost every new mother has to endure. Grin and bear them. They won't be fun, but they won't last long either.

- You've delivered the baby and the placenta, so the contractions should stop, right? Wrong. During the first few days, you'll feel contractions which help your uterus to return to its normal size. They can be painful, particularly if this wasn't your first delivery or if you were given Pitocin, a drug which stimulates contractions during or after delivery. The contractions will probably be most noticeable while you're nursing. Use your breathing and relaxation techniques and, with your doctor's permission, pain relievers. Other helpful measures are to lie on your stomach, take hot baths and keep your bladder empty.

- If you're so uncomfortable that you don't feel ready to go home after the minimum recommended hospital stay, talk to your insurance company and find out the maximum allowable length of stay. If you aren't ready to leave the hospital when the insurance company wants you to, talk to your doctor. She might be able to justify a longer stay based on your condition.

- When your breasts get hard as rocks, feel as big as boulders and hurt as if they were run over by a truck, you are experiencing engorgement. You might even get a low-grade fever, feel hot or flushed, and have sensations of fullness, tenderness and warmth in your breasts. As uncomfortable as it can be, it's a good thing. It means that your milk is coming in. As with most nursing-related discomforts, the best solution is to keep nursing. (If you're not nursing, see below.) For additional information on nursing and its effects on your body, look in Section Four.

- A well-fitting, supportive bra can help reduce your breast discomfort. You can even wear it at night.

- If you're not nursing, a tight-fitting support bra, worn day and night, can be helpful for you, too. Ice packs will help reduce the swelling. You can even take an analgesic to relieve your pain. If you're extremely uncomfortable, you can express a small amount of milk. Just remember that the amount of breast milk produced is based upon the demand. The more you express, the more you produce. The more you produce, the longer the drying up process will take.

- During the first week, when your lochia, the bloody vaginal discharge, is still heavy, it might collect in the back of your vagina when you're sitting or lying down. Don't be alarmed if you feel a sudden gush of fluid when you stand up.

CHAPTER SIX

The First Six Weeks After Childbirth

Recovering From Pregnancy

Everyone, regardless of how they delivered, goes through some attention-getting physical sensations during the first six post-partum weeks. The changes your body experiences during this time tend to be fairly dramatic as your uterus returns to normal, your bladder recovers, your hormones adjust and you get rid of all the extra fluid you've been carrying around. Following is a preview of what you can expect and what you can do to make yourself more comfortable.

- Doctors usually say that you won't bleed vaginally for more than about two weeks. While it should slow down considerably after two weeks, many mothers have some bloody discharge, called lochia, for up to six or eight weeks. If you're concerned, talk to your doctor.

- Sometime during the first ten to twenty days after giving birth, you might discharge what seems like a lot of bright red blood compared to what your lochia has looked like. This occurs when the scar where the placenta was attached to the uterus sloughs off. If this heavy bleeding continues for more than a few hours, contact your doctor.

- You might sweat a lot during the first few weeks as your body eliminates a lot of pregnancy-related fluids. Don't worry if you wake up dripping wet in the middle of the night.

- Other common physical experiences during the first few weeks after delivery include the need to urinate frequently, which helps you eliminate pregnancy-related fluid from your body, and hot flashes, which are common with low estrogen levels. (Great—just what you need—a glimpse of what's to come with menopause!)

- If you have any concerns about your personal well-being, talk to your doctor. It's normal to have questions that didn't get answered just after delivery. After all, many of the most surprising and confusing physical side-effects of childbirth happen after a new mother has been released from the hospital. Doctors actually welcome phone calls so they can find out how you're doing during the first days and weeks at home.

- You might have gotten hemorrhoids during pregnancy or delivery. Luckily, most minor hemorrhoids will disappear on their own. Medicated pads and creams will help the symptoms. Stool softeners, used with your doctor's permission, might help, too. And, as you probably know, don't strain while on the toilet. You can expect hemorrhoids to subside considerably by six weeks after delivery. If your hemorrhoids are more serious and persistent, talk to your doctor.

- Any vericose veins which developed during pregnancy will usually disappear by about six weeks after delivery, when your blood volume has returned to normal.

- A physical exam scheduled six weeks after a vaginal delivery or two weeks after a c-section is fairly standard. However, if you feel that you want to be examined earlier, that's up to you. You can visit the doctor whenever you feel the need.

- Saying good-bye to your doctor after your post-partum exam can be a strange experience. After all those monthly and weekly visits, it seems strange not to go to the doctor for a whole year. You might feel let down, somewhat abandoned since no one is taking care of you anymore. After you go a few more weeks without being examined, I assure you, you won't miss it.

- If you have on-going concerns after your post-partum exam, schedule another appointment or call the doctor or her nurse. Just because your doctor says that she'll see you in a year at your regular gynecological appointment doesn't mean that you have to wait until then to get your questions or concerns addressed. We get so used to following the doctor's orders explicitly during pregnancy that sometimes we forget that we can make medical choices, too.

On-Going Recovery From a Cesarean

If you had a c-section, your body has more to do in the first six weeks after childbirth than just go through the immediate after-effects of delivery that were just described. In addition to those experiences and other post-pregnancy changes, you still have some more recuperation related to your delivery. Being careful during this critical time will help you feel better as soon as possible. Overdoing it will only make the recovery process longer.

- During the second week after delivery, you'll find that you're able to move around a little more quickly, but that major movements are still difficult. You might still need occasional pain medication. The challenge this week is not to do too much. Be careful not to overdo things one day or you'll feel the effects the next.

   My biggest problem in recovering from a c-section was that I was trying to act like normal as much as possible. I was trying so hard to do everything I had expected to be able to do for Lea, that I downplayed the fact that I had had abdominal surgery. Once I finally acknowledged that I just couldn't get up and do things, I relaxed and did only what was comfortable. My stress level went way down and I felt much better. (Diane)

- Through the third and fourth weeks, normal movement will be fairly comfortable, but you might experience twinges of pain and achiness in your abdomen. You'll be self-sufficient in most ways, more active and able pick up things that are a little heavier than the baby, but you should still be careful. If you move too much during the day, the incision might hurt at night. Continue to get help with heavy housework and driving.

- By the sixth week, you'll probably be back to a fairly normal activity level. Remember that "normal" doesn't mean being overly active, trying to make up for lost time. It means doing what you would regularly do in a day. You'll just have to slowly catch up on everything you didn't do during the past six weeks.

- Be sure to follow your doctor's instructions about what you can and can't do. There are good reasons why you shouldn't drive, vacuum or pick up anything heavier than the baby while you're recovering. You might feel capable of driving, for example, but if you were driving and got into an accident, the steering wheel could push right into your incision. Furthermore, in that situation, your insurance might not cover you if you were acting against doctor's orders.

CHAPTER SEVEN

The Months After Childbirth

Changes in Your Body

Along with weight loss and getting back in shape (which you're probably
sick of thinking about but I'm going to talk about anyway), there are a lot
of other physical changes that happen during the months after childbirth.
These aren't the dramatic medical concerns that doctors and other new
moms tend to talk about, but they can surprise and worry you if you're
not anticipating them. Other than exercising to get back in shape, there's
not much you can do to address these body changes. It just helps you feel
better to know that what you're experiencing is normal.

- Your hair didn't fall out as quickly when you were pregnant as it does
  when you aren't. Now that you don't have all those pregnancy
  hormones, you'll lose all the hairs with life spans that expired while you
  were pregnant. This process can last up to six months.

  *After Claire was born, I found that I was even losing eyebrow and
  eyelash hairs!* (Taneesha)

- You might experience a decreased level of vaginal moisture, particularly
  if you're nursing. This dryness is caused by a decreased level of the
  hormone estrogen. (Yes, this is another preview of menopause!) When
  your estrogen level rises, the situation will return to normal.

- As pregnancy-related hormones decrease, you can expect the dark line
  between your belly button and pubic hair and the "mask of pregnancy,"

48

the darker coloration that may have appeared on your face, to disappear gradually.

- Some women find that their complexions get better when they're pregnant. Others find they get worse. After they deliver, some women find that their complexions return to a normal, pre-pregnant state. Others find that their complexions improve or get worse after delivery. There's just no predicting what will happen.

- One thing that might not change are your stretch marks. They'll get lighter over time, but they probably won't disappear completely.

- There's no way to predict exactly when your period will return. If you don't nurse, it might return six to eight weeks after giving birth. If you nurse, it usually returns six months to a year after giving birth. Remember, you may have ovulated even if you haven't gotten your period yet. Use birth control if you don't want to get pregnant again.

- Many women find that they experience fewer, less intense menstrual cramps after having given birth and that their menstrual flow is different in quantity and quality. Some women who previously had been somewhat irregular find that their schedule becomes more regular. The degree to which you're affected by Pre-Menstrual Syndrome (PMS) might also change—maybe for the better, maybe for the worse.

- You never know what size your breasts will be in their post-pregnant, post-nursing state. Some women stay larger. Others feel smaller and/or less firm than before. It can take some experimentation with both cup size and bra size to find a comfortable fit after your breasts find their new normal.

- There's an old wives' tale about women gaining a half shoe size per pregnancy. The story is old, but for many women it's true. Pregnancy-related swelling might be long gone, but your feet may stay larger anyway.

- It's common for women to experience numbness, itching or sensitivity on or around a c-section scar for months after delivery.

- As you already know, the best way to regain your figure is to exercise and eat right. Talk to your doctor before you start exercising. If you had an uncomplicated delivery, she will probably tell you to use your own judgment about when to resume—or begin—an exercise program. If your delivery was more difficult, she might have specific guidelines.

- You might find that your abdomen stays somewhat distended for months, especially if you had a c-section. Unless you make an effort to exercise your abdominal muscles, the condition might be permanent, regardless of whether or not you lose all the weight you gained during your pregnancy. Ask you doctor for some exercises or use the following suggestions.

- When you're ready to begin exercising, the exercises described below are fast and easy and can be done in the privacy of your own home.

I do sit-ups with Alex on my lap. It makes my exercise a fun time for both of us. (Madeline)

Easy Exercises

Start with a comfortable number of each of these exercises. As you get stronger, gradually increase the number you do during each exercise session.

SIDE BENDS: Stand with your legs spread at hip's width. Reach one hand over your head and bend to the opposite side as if you're reaching to touch the floor with the outstretched arm. Use the muscles on the side with the outstretched arm to pull yourself back up to a stand. Do a set of side bends on one side, then switch to the other.

PELVIC TILT: Stand with your knees bent slightly. Contract your abdominal muscles to tilt your pelvis toward the back. If you aren't sure you're doing this correctly, stand against a wall and practice using your abdominal muscles to flatten the small of your back against the wall. This exercise can also be done while you're lying on your back or on your hands and knees.

STOMACH CRUNCHES: Lie on the floor, on your back, with your knees bent. Place your hands behind your head with your elbows out and arms parallel to the floor. Use your upper abdominal muscles to lift your shoulders up off the floor. Your chin should stay pointed toward the ceiling. Exhale each time you curl up. Be careful that your lower back is pressed to the floor and that you're keeping your stomach muscles firm. If you're using your arms to pull you up, your neck will hurt and your stomach won't get flatter. Don't bounce against the floor to help you curl up, either.

- Walking is a terrific way to get in shape. If you push your baby in his stroller while you walk, you get exercise, plus it's a great way to meet other new moms. It can also be a great way for you and your partner to have some relaxing time together. Of course, a treadmill works, too, if you prefer to walk inside.

- You can also enroll in an exercise class specially designed for new mothers at a gym, recreation center or community center. This will give you exercise plus opportunities to meet other new moms.

- If you can't seem to get to your athletic club, but you like working out on a stationary bike, stair master or weight machine, you might want to consider purchasing a piece of equipment. The cost of many months of club membership might be equal to the cost of buying what you need.

- Post-natal exercise videos are another great choice if you like to exercise at home. Some even involve both you and your baby. You can use them as your sole source of exercise or just when you don't have the time or energy to leave the house for exercise.

- Try not to make weighing yourself or trying on your regular clothes a daily obsession. Weight loss doesn't happen at a consistent pace. You'll probably have days just after delivery when you lose a few pounds at once. Later, you may go for weeks without losing anything. Most women take six months or more to lose all their pregnancy weight.

- Even if you've returned to your pre-pregnancy weight, the pounds might be arranged a little differently. Common changes include broader hips, a rounder abdomen (your abdominal muscles are less taut than they used to be) and a thicker torso (your rib cage expanded to allow for the growing baby but didn't contract back).

Making Yourself Comfortable

It's important that you take care of your personal comfort, not just your physical health, during your first year of motherhood. While the small discomforts related to daily life aren't as obvious as the physical changes related to pregnancy and childbirth, they can get in the way of enjoying yourself and your baby. In most cases, all it takes to make yourself more comfortable is some advance planning and attention to details.

- New mothers often develop sore shoulders, necks or backs. Carrying the baby, the diaper bag and the other necessary paraphernalia stresses your muscles. Ask your doctor or a physical trainer for exercises to strengthen these areas. Also try to alternate the side on which you carry the baby and the diaper bag. This problem will lessen over time as your body gets stronger, but it's also a good idea to lighten your loads as much as possible. Make more than one trip to load and unload the car, eliminate unnecessary items from your diaper bag and carry only a small bag of essentials around with you. Leave the big, well-stocked diaper bag in the car.

- A massage, whether from a professional or your partner, is a wonderful way to relax tense muscles. It also can relieve some of the emotional and physical stress that caused them.

- Watch your posture. You might be hunching over while you nurse, bottle-feed, hold or even feed the baby while she's in the high chair. It might not bother you now, but it could lead to a sore back and on-going posture problems later. Adjust the height of the baby seat or select a different place to sit to encourage better posture.

- Don't assume every chair is the same. Test various chairs or couches to determine the most comfortable places to sit while you nurse, bottle-feed or spoon-feed the baby.

- It's easy to get so focused on taking care of your sick baby that you don't notice how you feel. When you take a sick baby to the doctor, ask her to check you for the same symptoms. If your baby's doctor is a pediatrician, she can't treat you, since you're an adult, but she can confirm the need for you to consult your own doctor. Even if you feel fine, you might be carrying around the same infection or sore throat. If you don't take care of yourself, who will take care of the baby—especially if you pass the cold or virus back and forth between you?

- Keep the baby's fingernails trimmed. Otherwise, he may not be the only one who ends up getting scratched.

- Keep an extra shirt in the trunk of your car or in your diaper bag. Even if it doesn't match what you're wearing, you'll be happy to have it when you're out of the house and your baby throws up or a messy diaper leaks all over you.

- Whenever possible, don't tempt fate by wearing dry-clean-only clothes when you're with your baby. You'll probably end up regretting it.

- Dress yourself as warmly in cold weather as you do your baby. If you tend to forget to bring a jacket for yourself, leave an extra one in your car. If you don't have a car, keep your coat in the same place you keep the diaper bag so you remember to bring it, too.

  Whenever I got ready to take Annika out in cold weather, I thought about getting the car warmed and all her stuff loaded before I pulled out of the garage. There were many times when it wasn't until I got out of the car at wherever I was going before I realized that I didn't have my own gloves or hat. Sometimes I'd even forgotten my coat. (Tiffany)

- Remember to eat and drink enough—especially, but not only, if you're nursing. You might spend so much time at the table feeding the baby that you forget to feed yourself until your stomach growls fifteen minutes after you leave the house.

- Pack snacks for yourself in the diaper bag.

- Remember to pack feminine supplies in your purse or diaper bag.

- Go to the bathroom when the urge hits—don't hold it. There might not be a convenient time to go for hours, so you might as well go when you need to. The baby will be okay for a few minutes, even if you have to put off feeding him until you're ready.

Having Sex

No matter what you look like, you should be proud, not ashamed, of your body. You and your partner saw the dramatic changes that took place with pregnancy and witnessed the incredible demands put on it by labor and delivery. It's important to acknowledge the physical side effects of childbirth as you start having sex again. Birth control should also be a major consideration. Hopefully, though, the rewards of slowly and carefully easing back into sex will be fulfilling for both you and your partner!

- Pay attention to your body's signals. Most doctors suggest waiting at least six weeks before having sex, but you might be ready a bit before or well after that time frame. Keep your doctor's instructions in mind, though. Having intercourse too soon after giving birth can be dangerous to your health.

- There are some fairly dramatic physical reasons why sex might not be terribly appealing to you right now. Milk leaks from your breasts when you get sexually aroused. The muscle tone around your vagina has changed temporarily. Your hormones are in chaos. You're in almost constant physical contact with your baby. You still may be sore from delivery. You're exhausted, too. I assure you and your partner that once these conditions subside a bit, your sex drive will probably return. If it doesn't, you could have an hormonal imbalance. Talk with your doctor.

- If intercourse isn't appealing to you for a while, pretend you're on a date. It can be fun trying to remember everything you did before you went all the way.

- Remember, being sensual can be as much fun as being sexual. Encourage your partner to enjoy exploring your full breasts and round hips. Massage each other, focusing on the muscles that are receiving a workout from carrying the baby. Have fun and be creative!

- Before you start having intercourse again, talk about birth control. After the months you spent trying to get pregnant (or not trying not to), nine months of pregnancy and six weeks or so of post-partum recovery, this might seem like a strange subject. However, since you won't know when you're ovulating until you start having your period on a regular basis, you need to address the issue.

- Breast-feeding is not a method of birth control!

  I got pregnant two months after my twins, Jack and Elissa, were born. Trust me: nursing won't keep you from getting pregnant! (Miranda)

- Even if high-tech medical intervention was involved in getting pregnant last time, you should assume that you could possibly conceive a baby from unprotected sex, unless there's a medically documented reason why you can't. Use birth control if you wouldn't welcome another pregnancy right now.

- Birth control options that you previously hadn't considered might be more attractive now. Options that were once appropriate might no longer suit your needs. Examine your own feelings and talk with your partner and doctor to help you make the best choice.

- Remember that the birth control method you choose to use while you're still sore or nursing doesn't have to be what you stay with.

- Many new parents find that they have a whole new appreciation for birth control. Before you planned on having a baby (assuming you did plan it), getting pregnant might not have been the end of the world. Now that you have a baby, you probably don't want to have another one right away. On the other hand, if your pregnancy was unplanned, you already know how important birth control is!

- The first few times you have sex might be a little bit painful or uncomfortable. Try the following ways to make it better.

What to Try: To Make Your First Post-Partum Sexual Intercourse More Comfortable

USE LUBRICATION, such as K-Y Jelly®. Don't use Vaseline.® It's ineffective as a lubricant and can cause problems with some birth control methods.

INDULGE IN A LOT OF FOREPLAY.

ENCOURAGE YOUR PARTNER TO BE EXTRA SLOW and gentle.

USE A FINGER TO TEST for discomfort before actually trying intercourse.

CHOOSE A POSITION, such as you being on top, in which you're in control of how much penetration is made.

PUT A PILLOW under you to elevate your hips if you're on the bottom.

HAVE INTERCOURSE WITHOUT FULL PENETRATION. Ask your partner to avoid making contact with your cervix.

IF YOU HAD A C-SECTION, REMIND YOUR PARTNER NOT TO REST HIS WEIGHT on your abdomen.

- The first few times you have sex might not be terribly satisfying for you, but any discomfort should lessen. If it doesn't, wait a week or two, then try again. If sex continues to be uncomfortable, talk to your doctor.

- Physical issues aren't all that affect your sexual desire and satisfaction. For more information on the numerous emotional factors, see the section on Your Sex Life starting on page 114 of Chapter 15.

Section Four

Enjoying Nursing

Feeding the baby is one of the first and most important responsibilities of a new mother. For many expectant moms, there's no question that nursing is the right choice for them. Others aren't as comfortable with the idea of nursing and want to consider bottle-feeding. Some women are absolutely sure they don't want to nurse.

No matter how you felt about it when you were pregnant, giving birth will probably make you feel more positive about nursing. So, if there's even the smallest chance you might want to nurse, I strongly recommend that you try it. Although it may seem strange and difficult at first, you and your baby will probably get the hang of it within a few days.

Now that I've said that I think you should at least try nursing, I also want to remind you that nursing isn't an all or nothing proposition. One of the best aspects of nursing is its flexibility. The choice about how often to nurse and how long to continue to nurse is always yours and always available to you. Once your milk supply is established and your baby is nursing well (which may happen as soon as the first few weeks), you can nurse as much or as little as you want, as long as you're fairly consistent about it. There's nothing wrong with supplementing nursing with bottles or cups of formula or breast milk some of the time. In fact, if supplementing helps you feel better about continuing to nurse at all, it's actually a good thing to do.

No matter how long you plan on nursing, you'll find that it's worth making the effort to get off to a good start. If you have a positive attitude, set realistic expectations and establish effective nursing techniques, you'll be comfortable and satisfied with nursing. When you enjoy nursing, you'll be more successful at it. That doesn't mean that you still won't have times when you feel like you're just a feeding machine, but they'll happen less frequently.

CHAPTER EIGHT

Deciding Whether to Nurse or Bottle-Feed

You're the only one who can nurse your baby. Because nursing has such a large impact on your body and your lifestyle, you have to be happy with your choices about whether to nurse in the first place and how long to continue to nurse. Both decisions are important for you as well as your baby. As you make these choices, it's important to think about the pros and cons for both of you, in the short-term and the long-term. Whatever you choose to do is fine, as long as you've done what's right for you and your baby.

- Different babies take to nursing differently. Different mothers take to nursing differently. Just because your best friend hated nursing, doesn't necessarily mean that you will. Your experiences of nursing your first baby won't necessarily recur with the second. All you can do is consider how you feel at the time your baby is born. Acknowledge your feelings, then be true to them.

    When I became pregnant the second time, I was thrilled with everything but the prospect of nursing. I had nursed Chase for two and a half months. I never had any problems with nursing and loved the closeness with him, but didn't love the fact that every nursing session took over an hour. He was just a slow eater. I was surprised and thrilled when Charlie could finish a nursing session in ten minutes or less. This time I found that I loved the experience. I nursed him twice as long as I had nursed Chase and missed it when it was over. (Lynne)

I was really nervous about nursing, but I wanted to at least try it. I had a hard time getting started, but after a few visits with the hospital's lactation specialist, I was more confident. Within a couple of weeks, nursing became the easiest, most natural thing in the world. Other than a few bouts of sore nipples, I had no more problems and found nursing to be convenient and rewarding. I nursed Maya for fourteen months, at which point she weaned herself. (Holly)

• When you're deciding whether to nurse or to bottle-feed your baby consider the following:

BENEFITS OF BREASTMILK: Breastmilk automatically adjusts to the changing nutritional needs of your baby, has a complete and easily absorbable combination of nutrients, provides protection against infections and may help minimize the baby's tendency toward certain allergies. While formula is nutritious, it cannot match these unique qualities of breastmilk.

YOUR HEALTH: AIDS, chronic medical conditions which require certain medications, previous surgery or damage to your breasts can make it unsafe or impossible for you to nurse.

YOUR BABY'S HEALTH: Metabolic disorders or physical problems, such as a cleft palate, might affect whether you can or should nurse your baby.

ACTIVITY LEVEL: If you're uncomfortable about nursing in public places, you might need to cut back your activity level or bottle-feed when you're out of the house. If you'll be away from your baby frequently, for work or other activities, you need to consider how you want to balance nursing and bottle-feeding or whether you want to use only bottles.

COST: Nursing is virtually free. Bottle-feeding paraphernalia and formula can be expensive.

CONVENIENCE: For some moms, nursing is more convenient because there's no preparation. The milk is always there and ready. For others, bottle-feeding is more convenient because they don't always have to be the one to feed the baby. It's also nice because other people can share the responsibilities and pleasures of feeding her. An added convenience is that once the baby can hold her own bottle, she'll be able to feed herself.

PERSONAL PREFERENCE: If you desperately want to have your body back as your own, bottle-feeding might be the best option. If you love having a physical connection to your baby, nursing is for you.

> *The idea of nursing in front of other people made me very nervous. I was so worried about being embarrassed that I wasn't sure I should nurse. After going through the indignities of labor and delivery, I was surprised to find that nursing seeming so functional that I wasn't as upset about some breast showing as I thought I'd be. I cover myself up more than some women do, but I'm comfortable nursing anywhere.* (Shelley)

- Nipple shape and breast size are not factors that affect whether or not you can breast-feed your baby. If you have inverted nipples or extremely large breasts, you may have to take a few extra steps to prepare your nipples or correctly position your baby at the breast, but you can still be successful once you get used to it.

- If you choose not to nurse, it should be because of your personal feelings and preferences, not because you're having difficulty getting started. Lots of moms who nurse successfully had a hard time at first. If you want to nurse your baby even though you're having problems now, get help from a lactation consultant. To find one, contact the women's education service or the obstetrics unit at a hospital, call La Leche League (look in the white pages) for a referral or look in the yellow pages under "breast-feeding." You may also find advertisements for lactation specialists in local parenting magazines and newspapers. With a little coaching and lots of practice, you'll probably be able to nurse your baby.

- If you're leaning against nursing because you're afraid you'll get stuck doing it more often or for a longer period of time than you want to, you can stop worrying and start taking steps to avoid that problem. If you know you want to use bottles at some point, I strongly encourage you to ignore advice about waiting until your baby is six weeks old so she won't get "nipple confusion." The only babies I've seen having trouble taking a bottle were ones who weren't given one until they were older than six weeks. As long as your milk is coming in strong and your newborn is nursing well, you can start supplementing with bottles of breastmilk or formula as soon as you want to. Once your baby takes a bottle, you have a lot of flexibility about how often she is breast-fed and how long you continue to nurse.

- No matter what the reason, if it's a choice between not nursing at all or supplementing nursing with bottles, I suggest you supplement. You always have the option of switching completely to bottle-feeding if you take the second option. If you decide not to nurse, there's no changing your mind after the first few days. Well, there are ways, but they're complicated. Just ask your doctor!

- Keep the flexible aspect of breast-feeding in mind as you decide whether or not to nurse your baby. Once nursing is well established, you can do it as much or little as you want. Many mothers, for example, nurse their babies first thing in the morning and just before bedtime at night and give a bottle or cup the rest of the time. As long as you stay fairly consistent about how often you breast-feed, your milk supply will adjust accordingly.

- Even if you only nurse for a short time, your baby will get the benefits of your colostrum, the fluid in your breasts before the milk comes in, as well as your milk.

- If you're still undecided about whether or not to nurse, it might help to list your personal pros and cons of the various aspects of nursing and bottle-feeding. But if you get to the end and you're still uncertain, I suggest you opt for nursing.

- Don't feel guilty if nursing doesn't feel like the best choice for you. A mother who hates nursing, but does it anyway, ends up spending six hours or more a day doing something she dislikes. If you aren't happy nursing, don't do it. While the American Academy of Pediatrics says breast milk is best, today's formulas are a very safe alternative for most babies. It's better to be a happy mother who gives her baby a bottle than to be an unhappy mother who nurses only out of a sense of guilt.

I nursed Emilie for one and a half weeks. That's all I could stand physically and mentally. Emilie had such a strong sucking mechanism that the nurses in the maternity ward nicknamed her "The Barracuda." I was bleeding, in pain and very tense each time she was ready to eat. I finally switched to pumping, an exponentially more comfortable process. I was happy that I was following everyone's "breastmilk is best" advice. Then, reality hit me: I was spending every waking moment (or what seemed like ninety-nine hours a day at that point) either pumping, sterilizing equipment, feeding the baby or washing bottles and nipples . . . among the other "new baby" activities. I was going nuts because I couldn't leave the house. At that point I set out to take a survey of health care professionals to try to confirm my mother's advice that, "Formula is O.K. You turned out fine on Similac®." Well, the nurses in the maternity ward, the nurses at the pediatrician's office, the baby books I had and even the American Academy of Pediatrics all supported the "nursing is best at all costs" theory. It made me feel incredibly guilty for even considering the formula idea. I finally took my mother's advice, stopped driving myself crazy and proceeded with the formula. Emilie was fine, I was fine, my husband was fine and life was a whole lot better.
(Sallie)

CHAPTER NINE

Starting to Nurse

Mentally Adjusting to Being a Nursing Mom

Nursing your baby, especially if you aren't supplementing with bottles, is a huge responsibility. Your schedule will revolve around his needs. Your body won't be yours alone. Although your baby's nutritional needs are the primary concern, you're likely to grow increasingly frustrated with the whole process of nursing if that's all you think about. If you want to avoid feeling like a feeding machine, you have to acknowledge and respect your feelings about how nursing affects you and the choices you make. Use the tips in this section to help you find ways to make nursing satisfying and rewarding for both you and your baby.

- Nursing can feel awkward, embarrassing and downright unnatural the first few days. This is a very normal first reaction. Don't assume that you made the wrong choice about how to feed your baby.

- Lots of new moms are nervous about nursing. What if the baby has a hard time latching on? How will you know if she's is getting enough? Try to relax and see what happens. Remember that it can take several weeks for nursing to get well established. You aren't expected to be an immediate expert at something you've never done before.

- Although breast-feeding is a natural process, knowing exactly how to do it might not come naturally. If you want to nurse, but are having problems, don't give up. Read books on breast-feeding, talk to La Leche

League representatives or a lactation consultant, ask questions of your doctor, seek advice from other moms—do whatever it takes to fix the problems. And keep trying to nurse while you're at it! (If your baby doesn't seem to be thriving—she's too tired to eat or isn't wetting many diapers—consult with her pediatrician.)

- Nursing isn't a test of motherhood. Successful breast-feeding doesn't depend only on you, either. Remember that it takes practice for both mother and baby to get nursing well established.

- Acknowledge how your feelings about nursing change over time. There are bound to be some fluctuations in your emotions and your experiences. Some days it feels perfectly natural and rewarding. Other times it's frustrating and embarrassing. In the early days, remind yourself that your baby is learning a new skill, too. Nursing will become easier with practice. Later on, when you occasionally wish that you had your body back, re-evaluate your options and make choices that are appropriate for the current situation.

- While nursing seems to take an inordinate amount of thought and preparation for the first couple of weeks, it will quickly become easy and natural. Before long, you'll probably be able to do it without even thinking about it.

   Once Taylor and I got used to nursing, I was surprised to find myself feeling exhilarated and powerful about my ability to provide her with nourishment and comfort. It's an incredibly wonderful sensation, especially after feeling so frustrated with it at first. (Caryn)

- If you're embarrassed about nursing in front of certain people, such as your father-in-law or your partner's college buddies, there's nothing wrong with turning your chair away or excusing yourself and leaving the room. Conversely, if you're comfortable nursing in front of other people, but they aren't, they can turn away or excuse themselves, especially if they're in your home.

- When you have a particularly difficult nursing session, seek privacy, put the baby down, relax and start all over again. Most likely, you'll both be better able to get started this time.

- Remember that you have options if nursing starts to cause more physical discomfort or mental anxiety than you can handle. You can either breast-feed less often and use bottles or completely switch to bottle-feeding. It's important that your baby has a happy mother. Bottle-feeding in this situation might help your ability to bond with your baby and feel more fulfilled in your new role.

Getting Your Breasts Ready to Nurse

As a breast-feeding mother, your breasts, not your uterus, are now your baby's life support system. Your breasts need to adapt to their new status as the rest of your body recovers from pregnancy and childbirth. The first few days or weeks while your nipples and breasts are adjusting to their new responsibilities can be difficult for some, but not all, new mothers.

Luckily, once you get used to nursing, your breasts will automatically adjust to meet your baby's needs. Nursing will become an easy and enjoyable process that takes hardly any thought or preparation.

- To bring out an inverted or flat nipple so the baby can latch on, gently stimulate your nipple with your fingers. If that doesn't work, mist the nipple with cold water. An alternative is to apply an ice cube wrapped in a washcloth or gauze squares that were dampened, then put in the freezer to be used as needed. Another option is to use a breast pump just long enough to pull the nipple out.

- For the first few days after your baby's birth, your breasts will be filled with colostrum, an early form of milk that has numerous benefits for your new baby. Within a few days, your milk will come in. Your breasts may become extremely swollen and painful. This is normal! Nurse frequently, even if it's uncomfortable for you.

- If your baby has trouble latching on because your breasts are so engorged (full and hard) that your nipples are almost flat, try expressing a bit of milk by hand or with a pump before you let the baby nurse. Warm showers and gentle massage may help you reduce the discomfort and get the milk flowing. Don't worry. It won't always be like this. Your breasts will soon adjust and produce the amount of milk your baby needs.

I knew I was going to get engorged when my milk came in, but I thought that just meant I would get very full. I had actually been looking forward to having a large chest! I had no idea it would hurt so much. I was so focused on nursing through the pain that I didn't even get to enjoy being big! (Lindsay)

I was so full that my milk was squirting out too fast and gagging Anna. I learned to express some milk by hand to release the pressure before she started to nurse. (Marianne)

- Don't delay or avoid nursing because you know it's going to hurt. The best way to help your breasts toughen up is to nurse more often, not less. If you don't nurse enough to drain your breasts, there could be more painful consequences later on, including breast infections.

What to Try: To Encourage Milk Let-Down

Sometimes the milk is there, but it's not flowing easily. You can use the following tips to help you get it started.

RELAX. Try using your Lamaze breathing or other relaxation techniques.

APPLY WARM COMPRESSES to your breasts for about five minutes before you start nursing.

TAKE A HOT SHOWER just before the nursing session.

MASSAGE YOUR BREASTS, starting from the top and rubbing in long, gentle, vertical strokes toward the nipples.

VISUALIZE THE MILK RUSHING to your nipples.

STIMULATE YOUR NIPPLES with your hand.

LET THE BABY START TO SUCK. Don't do this for long if the milk isn't there or you'll get sore.

THINK ABOUT SOMETHING CALM and relaxing. You might be thinking about nursing so much that you're creating a problem rather than avoiding one.

USE A BREAST PUMP until the milk starts to flow.

DRINK SOMETHING WARM.

TALK TO YOUR DOCTOR if you're having extreme difficulty with let-down. Hormone treatments might be appropriate for you.

- Let-down can hurt when you first start a nursing session. It feels like sharp, poking pains in your breasts. Don't worry. What you're feeling is a good thing since it means that milk is flowing from the milk glands down to your nipples. As soon as it gets there, the feeling will go away.

- Once you're used to nursing and your milk supply is well-established, the sharp sensation of let-down, the spontaneous dripping of milk and the feeling of fullness will probably diminish or even disappear. These are good signs, not signs that your milk production has dropped. If your baby is happy and healthy, everything's fine. Enjoy the fact that nursing has gotten easier and more comfortable.

CHAPTER TEN

Good Nursing Habits

Taking Care of Your Breasts

Taking care of your breasts will be practically effortless once you and your baby learn to breast-feed. In the meantime, however, you must take action immediately while continuing to nurse if your nipples or breasts become sore. Ignoring these problems will not make them go away.

- The number one, most important tip about breast care is that the solution to almost every nursing problem is to keep nursing. It's a good idea to nurse even more frequently if you're having problems. Just make sure to position the baby properly and take good care of your breasts.

- Alternate the side on which you start each nursing session. This will ensure each of your breasts makes the same amount of milk and drains fully several times a day. This keeps you from getting lop-sided and from getting breast infections.

- It's a challenge to remember which breast to start on at each nursing session, particularly if the one you should start on doesn't feel fuller. This sounds like a stupid thing to worry about until you're sitting there at 5:00 am trying to remember what happened during the 2:00 am feeding. All the feeding sessions may become a blur in your memory. The old trick of putting a diaper pin (if you can still find one of these old-fashioned objects) on the side of your bra is one option. Writing it down is another. You can work out your own signal. Just be sure that you're always consistent about whether the signal indicates the side to start on

69

What to Try: To Prevent Sore Nipples

POSITION THE BABY so that she is sucking, but not pulling on you.

PLACE MOST OF THE AREOLA, not just the nipple, in the baby's mouth.

REPOSITION THE BABY if he latches on improperly—even if he has already started to nurse.

NEVER PULL YOUR BABY'S MOUTH OFF your nipple. Use your finger to break the suction when your baby has finished nursing, but is still sucking. Gently press your down on your breast just outside the baby's mouth.

RUB LANOLIN CREAM ON YOUR NIPPLES after nursing. Don't use lanolin, however, if you're allergic to wool. Be sure to rub the lanolin off the baby's lips after nursing or it might create a gummy build-up. Don't be surprised if your dog goes crazy trying to sniff your breasts or lick the baby's face. Dogs love the taste of lanolin.

ALTERNATE THE SIDE ON WHICH YOU START NURSING. Babies suck harder at first. If you always start on the same side, that side might get more sore. By the way, it's also important to alternate which side you start on so one breast doesn't start making more milk than the other, leaving you lopsided.

NURSE REGULARLY so both your baby and your breasts will adjust to the process of nursing.

LET YOUR NIPPLES DRY before closing your bra.

USE A FRESH NURSING PAD after every feeding.

RINSE YOUR NIPPLES WITH WATER when you bathe. You don't need soap, which might irritate or dry out your nipples.

this time or the side you used first last time. I guarantee that it won't be a problem if you occasionally mess up, just don't make it a habit. If you can't remember which side you started on last time, pick one for this time. Then try hard to remember for the next time.

- If you have an area of your breast that feels hot and tender, you might have a blocked duct that is causing inflammation, called mastitis. Please don't stop nursing! That will only make your problem worse. In fact, encourage your baby to nurse enough to completely drain the milk ducts in that breast. Because the blocked duct may be caused by the baby not latching on correctly, change the way you hold the baby while he nurses. Also put warm compresses on the area as frequently as practical. Hot showers will help, too. If the problem persists, talk to your doctor.

- If you have breast tenderness that isn't relieved by nursing, your breast is red and you have a fever, feel chilled or have flu-like symptoms, you might have a breast infection. Talk to your doctor, but keep nursing.

What to Try: To Relieve Sore Nipples

NURSE YOUR BABY MORE FREQUENTLY, for shorter periods of time.

TRY A DIFFERENT POSITION for the baby. This might help reduce the amount of suction put on sore areas. (See the next section in this chapter.)

POSITION YOURSELF DIFFERENTLY when you nurse.

START THE NURSING SESSION WITH THE LEAST SORE BREAST.

REMOVE THE BABY FROM YOUR BREAST as soon as she's done eating.

RUB A FEW DROPS OF BREASTMILK into your nipples after each feeding, then allow them to air dry.

USE WASHABLE CLOTH NURSING PADS instead of disposable, plastic-backed ones.

USE HARD PLASTIC BREASTS SHIELDS inside your bra. These shields prevent your bra from rubbing on your skin and allow air to circulate around your nipples.

MAKE SURE THAT YOUR OLDER BABY'S MOUTH IS FREE OF FOOD before nursing.

TAKE YOUR BABY AND YOURSELF TO THE DOCTOR if he has thrush, a yeast infection that results in white patches in his mouth that can't be rubbed off.

Holding the Baby So You're Comfortable

Your baby's only specific positioning need is that you keep her head at least a little bit higher than the rest of her body while she's nursing. All the other aspects of holding the baby properly have more to do with your comfort than hers. If you're not careful about how you position her, you could have some physical pain and discomfort as well as potentially cause an infection. The following suggestions will help you avoid problems as you learn to nurse. You won't have to worry about it for long, though. As your baby gets older and your body recovers from delivery and becomes accustomed to holding the weight of the baby, positioning issues will become less important.

- Bring the baby to the breast, not the breast to the baby. Place a pillow under your arm to help support the nursing baby. This will bring her up to the appropriate level and ensure that you don't hunch over.

  As a shower gift, I was given a contoured pillow for babies to lie and play on. Instead of waiting to use it when Blake was old enough to play on it, I used it as a nursing pillow. The pillow supported my arm and the contoured area cradled the baby. (Sherri)

- Use a footrest or ottoman to help you maintain the proper posture while you're nursing. This will also help you use your legs, not just your arms, to support the baby's weight.

- If you had a c-section, you'll probably be most comfortable if you use the football hold (with the baby's body tucked under your arm and her head facing your breast) or lie on your side until your incision heals. If you want to hold the baby across your lap while you nurse, place her on top of a pillow to raise her up and keep her from pressing on your abdomen.

- If you have large breasts, it's particularly important that you support the weight of your breast while you nurse. Cup your hand underneath it or wedge a small pillow under your arm and part of your breast. This will help your baby maintain a hold on the nipple and ensure that the milk ducts from the lower part of your breast are drained.

- Some women find it easier to hold the baby with their right hand while they position their left breast with the left hand, and vice versa. Then they switch hands to cradle the baby once he's latched on. Other women find it easier to use their left hand to hold the baby to the left breast while they position the nipple with their right hand, and vice versa. Experiment to see what's most comfortable for you. There's no right or wrong way to do it. Remember, your baby has never done this before either. Whatever you do will probably be fine with him.

CHAPTER ELEVEN

Nursing and the Rest of Your Body

Your breasts aren't the only parts of your body that are important to successful breast-feeding. The rest of you needs to be cared for, too. It's not at all selfish to take your physical comfort, health, and modesty into consideration. After all, if you're uncomfortable or embarrassed, you won't be relaxed and happy when you're nursing. The experience won't be a good one for either you or your baby.

- Before you start a nursing session, go to the bathroom, get something to drink, place the phone and TV remote control within reach, get a book or do whatever it takes for you to be comfortable while nursing. The baby will nurse better and you will enjoy the experience more if you aren't interrupted or restless.

- When you start nursing on one breast, the other breast might leak. Be sure to wear nursing pads and to keep fresh sets with you at all times.

- It's common to leak during the night, especially when your baby is just starting to sleep for longer periods. You might want to wear nursing pads and a bra at night. Another option is to sleep on a towel.

- If your breasts are very large, try wearing a bra at night, even if you aren't leaking. The extra support may make you more comfortable.

- If you're anxious to finally sleep on your stomach again, but find it difficult or uncomfortable to put pressure on your breasts, put a thin pillow under your stomach. This might lift you up enough to create a valley between your pillows for your breasts.

- If you start leaking when you're not getting ready to nurse the baby, cross your arms across your breasts and press. This not only hides the problem, but the pressure on your nipples will help stop the flow of milk.

  During the first few weeks after my milk came in, my breasts leaked so much that neither disposable nor cloth nursing pads could prevent milk from seeping through to my blouse. I was so desperate that I decided to try super absorbency sanitary pads. Half of a thin maxi pad in each bra cup took care of the problem. (Sharon)

  I needed a chest x-ray to check for pneumonia a couple of months after Nicholas was born. As soon as the paper medical gown touched my breasts, the milk started to flow. I leaked so much that it shredded the gown. The x-ray technician was great about it. He just said that it was wonderful that I had so much milk for my baby. (Debbie)

- Just thinking about your baby or hearing another baby cry may be enough to make your milk leak. Be sure to wear breast pads and be careful about what shirts you wear if this tends to happen to you.

  I had to go to a fancy event the week after Joe was born. My concern was finding something that fit, looked nice and didn't bother my c-section scar. It didn't occur to me to consider whether my breast pads showed through until I got there. I kept my arms crossed in front of me until my good friends reassured me that I was safe. After that, I added yet another criteria to my list of what to consider when choosing something to wear. (Carrie)

- Getting yourself dressed in the morning can be frustrating. Even though you're sick of maternity clothes, anxious to wear your regular wardrobe and tired of having to think about what you can wear, you still have to consider how appropriate each piece of clothing is for your new lifestyle. How easily you can access your breasts for nursing? Does it protect your modesty? Is it easily washed? Will breastmilk show up on it or stain it? Do you feel good about yourself when you wear it?

  We were having a large crowd of family and friends over for Zachary's bris, the Jewish ritual circumcision performed eight days after birth. This was the first time that I'd worn anything other than nightgowns and sweats since getting home from the hospital. Unfortunately, I was thinking more about how I looked and about not having my clothes rub

on my c-section scar than about my new role as a nursing mother. The dress I chose was high-necked and zipped up the back. I had to leave the party and get completely undressed in order to nurse him. No one other than my mother, sisters and best friends could visit with me while I was nursing because I was almost totally naked. (Sherri)

- Try on nursing bras before you purchase them. Not only should they be comfortable, but also easy to fasten and unfasten with one hand. Experiment with different closure styles (top of the cup, side of the cup, snaps, hooks, etc.) to determine what works best for you. Select bras that are machine washable. Or, if you're like me, much to my mother's dismay, you can machine wash them even if they aren't. Nursing bras typically aren't too dainty or delicate anyway, plus they'll probably get so stained and stretched that you won't want to wear them again even if you have another baby. Who cares what happens to them?

- When you choose clothes to wear while you're breast-feeding, remember that shirts which button up the front make for easy access, but unbuttoning from the top leaves the upper portion of your breast exposed while you nurse. Unbutton the shirt from the bottom for a more modest approach. Shirts that are loose can be pulled up and offer good coverage of your breasts, but leave your midriff exposed. Nursing shirts with a flap cover the baby's head and your breast while he's nursing.

- When you select shirts which are specially designed for nursing mothers, use only one hand to check how easy it is to fasten and unfasten any front flaps. Remember that you'll probably be holding the baby with the other hand.

- It's a good habit to have a glass of water or juice every time you sit down to nurse.

- Continue to take your prenatal vitamins while you're nursing.

- Limit your caffeine and alcohol intake. A little is okay, a lot isn't.

- No matter how much you want to lose weight, don't diet while you're nursing (unless you're under a doctor's care, of course). Starve yourself, starve your baby.

- Your body uses about eight hundred calories per day to produce enough milk for the average newborn baby. This is in addition to the number of calories you normally need. Since about two hundred to three hundred calories come from the fat you stored up during your pregnancy, you need about five hundred additional calories per day over your normal, non-pregnant calorie intake in order to produce adequate milk until you lose all your pregnancy weight. Once you've lost the weight, your daily calorie intake should be eight hundred calories more than normal.

- It's particularly important that you take special care of yourself while your baby experiences a growth spurt so you can meet your baby's increased nutritional demands. Drink extra fluids and eat nutritiously. Take naps, too, especially if your baby is waking frequently during the night.

- If your baby's doctor says your baby isn't gaining enough weight, but she's nursing well and emptying your breasts, you may not be producing enough milk. If you don't want to supplement with formula, take really good care of yourself to help you build up your milk supply. Rest more, drink more, eat more nutritiously, put off doing anything that can wait, and encourage your baby to eat every 3 hours or so, even if that means waking her up to eat. Focus on building up your milk supply for at least a few days. Within a week or two, this should produce results. If you still think your baby isn't being fully satisfied, talk to the doctor, La Leche League members, a lactation consultant and/or other nursing moms for additional suggestions.

- Keep nursing even when you're sick, unless your doctor tells you otherwise. In most cases, nursing will help keep your baby healthy. If you do need to go to a doctor, be sure to let her know that you're nursing so she can prescribe medication that is safe for both of you.

- Before taking any medications, over-the-counter or prescription, ask your doctor or pharmacist about their effects on nursing.

- The best time to take medication is just after you've finished nursing your baby. This allows your body time to absorb the medicine and reduces the amount that will be in your breastmilk.

CHAPTER TWELVE

Weaning

You probably spent so much time and effort establishing good nursing routines that it seems strange when you have to start thinking about completely weaning your baby from the breast. Luckily, you have lots of choices and flexibility in weaning, just as you did with nursing. You can probably ease into it and figure out what works for you and your baby. No matter how nervous this process makes you, remember that you've already established good feeding patterns once, when you started nursing. Now that you're ready to stop nursing, you can do it again.

- Even if you and your baby enjoy nursing, the time may come during the first year when you're ready to stop. Carefully evaluate the pros and cons of weaning so you can avoid, or at least minimize, any potential feelings of guilt. It may also be helpful to remind yourself about all the health benefits your baby received from your breastmilk, regardless of how long you nursed.

- If you know from the start that you won't be nursing for long, you might want to introduce your baby to a bottle within the first month. Some experts recommend waiting until your baby is at least six weeks old, but I've seen many moms follow this advice only to have the baby refuse the bottle. Once your baby is nursing well, it's probably safe to introduce a bottle. Even if she only has one bottle a day for a while, it will make weaning her from the breast much, much easier.

- Some people think babies should completely stop nursing at or soon after their first birthdays. If that works for you, that's great. If not, keep nursing. La Leche League is a wonderful resource and support group if you want support, encouragement and advice about nursing a toddler.

- Whatever choice you make about how long to nurse, make sure you're making decisions based on your own feelings, not other people's advice. Do what's right for you and your baby.

- Set a goal for when you want your baby to be completely weaned. Gradually ease into the process. It generally isn't something that can be accomplished all at once.

- Once your baby has learned to take a bottle or cup, you can gradually cut down on nursing. To do this, you need to cut down on two things: the number of nursing sessions each day and the amount the baby nurses during each session. Choose which one you want to reduce first. See how your baby reacts. If what you chose doesn't seem to be working, try the other alternative. Once you've successfully reduced either the number of times you nurse or the amount you nurse at each session, you need to start working on reducing the other.

- To start nursing less often, skip the times that are the most inconvenient for you to nurse, perhaps in the evening when you might want to go out without the baby or during the night when your partner could give her a bottle. Just make sure, for the sake of your own comfort, that you're consistent about which feedings are breast-feedings and which are for bottles, cups or food. Once you're down to only a few nursing sessions, cut back on how much you nurse at each session.

- You have options for reducing the amount you nurse at each feeding session. One is to cut back on how many minutes you nurse during each session, then finish the feeding with a bottle, cup or food. The other option is to start the feeding with something else, then offer your breast when your baby is full and won't want to nurse much. Once you're down to only a couple of minutes, you can start skipping some nursing sessions, then skipping entire days. Soon the days will add up and your baby will be completely weaned.

I got James down to one short nursing session just before he went to bed. We had been doing this for a few weeks. Then one night I went out for the evening. I came home just after his usual bedtime, expecting to nurse him, but found him sound asleep already. My husband said James ate dinner, played, then had a few ounces of water in a bottle and went to sleep without a fuss. The next night, I had to decide whether I was really ready to be done nursing. I decided that he was ready, even if I wasn't. But since it happened so easily, I went along with it. (Elaine)

- As you wean your baby from the breast, don't give in to the temptation to express a little milk between feedings to relieve the pressure. If you do, your body will only produce more milk, prolonging the whole process. Grit your teeth, use good nursing pads, avoid crowded places where someone could bump into your chest and hold your arms out away from your sides if your breasts are sensitive to pressure.

- As you begin to drop nursing sessions, be sure to wear nursing pads. You'll probably leak a lot until your milk production diminishes. If you do start to leak, press your arms against the sides of your breasts. This may slow or stop it.

- Once your baby is happily taking a bottle or cup, another option for complete weaning is to quit cold turkey. If you choose this option, do something drastic like leaving your baby with Dad or Grandma for a day, so you can't go back on your decision.

- Don't be surprised if you can express drops of milk for months after you stop nursing. It might take weeks after you stop nursing for your breasts to return to "normal," whatever that might be after going through pregnancy and nursing. Be careful not to run out and buy new bras or clothes too soon.

A few weeks after I stopped nursing Joey, I thought my breasts had returned to normal. I went out and bought a new bathing suit that had fairly firm cups in the bra. After a few months, those cups stood out on their own. My breasts didn't even touch them anymore. Sure, my chest was much smaller when I bought the suit than it had been when I was nursing full-time, but, since it had been over a year since my breasts had been in a non-pregnant, non-nursing state, I didn't remember what normal was. Maybe expecting to fill up that cup size was just wishful thinking, too. (Sheryl)

- Some women experience pain as their milk dries up. The location of the ache might be an indicator of which milk ducts are drying up. The discomfort should go away within a couple of weeks.

- You might find yourself feeling a bit sad about your baby being weaned —no more tiny, dependent baby. He seems so much older now that he can get a drink from anybody, anywhere. Don't worry, he still needs you in many other ways.

- On the other hand, there's nothing to be ashamed of if you're absolutely thrilled when it's time to wean your baby. Finally, you can have your body back! You also can have a lot more freedom your schedule.

I celebrated Taryn being weaned by going away with a girlfriend for the weekend. It was the first time in eight months that I had been away for more than five hours at a time. It felt like heaven! (Nina)

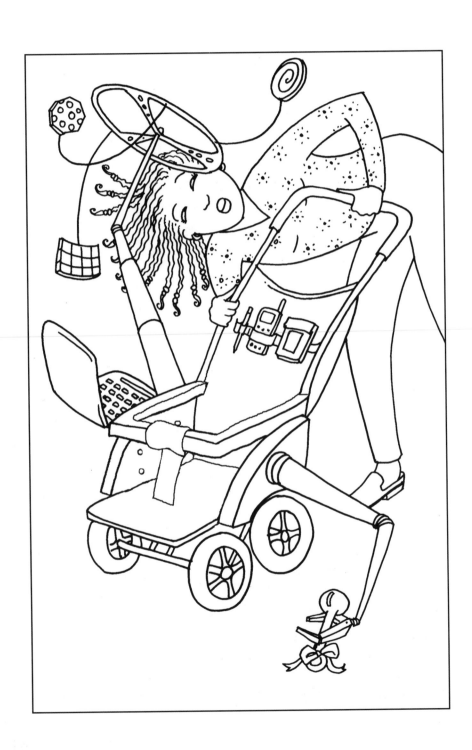

Section Five

Choosing the Right Baby Products

I'll admit that shopping for baby equipment and supplies isn't as emotional as adjusting to being a mother or as difficult as making career choices. It certainly isn't as hard to figure out what to buy as it is to learn how to breast-feed, find a child care provider or handle many of the responsibilities addressed in this book. In fact, you're probably looking forward to shopping for your baby.

You may be wondering why this section is here at all since shopping is usually fun, not stressful. Well, it's here because if you don't choose carefully, you could run into a whole lot of frustration later. The choices you make now can have a huge impact on your future convenience and comfort. What's more, they can affect your baby's happiness and safety. You can't just think about how something looks or how much it costs. You have to think about how it's designed and how it works.

It will help to keep the features listed in this section in mind as you select your baby equipment. Not all of these factors are equally important to everybody, however. Consider your lifestyle. For example, do you get around by taxi, bus, train or car? How big is the baby's room? How often do you anticipate taking your baby out in the stroller? Make the choices that will make your baby as safe and your life as easy as possible.

CHAPTER THIRTEEN

Deciding What You Need

What You Do and Don't Need

When you first become a mother, it seems as if you'll be using baby supplies and equipment forever. In reality, though, many stages with a baby only last a few months. When you know how long and in what ways different baby items are used, you can decide which items are important for you to have. Sometimes it's worth buying items that will make life a lot easier during a certain time period. Other times it's better to borrow. You might not need some of these items at all.

- It's easy to get caught up in wanting to "keep up with the Joneses." Try to stay focused on what you truly want and need rather than on what commercials or friends say you should have.

- As wonderful as baby equipment is, sometimes it just can't take the place of mommy's arms, daddy's lap or a soft blanket on the floor. Don't forget these low-tech options! (Unless you're in the car, of course, when you must use a car seat.)

- Your baby needs very little other than a safe place to sleep and a car seat. What you need depends solely on your lifestyle, parenting style and personal preferences. Don't feel guilty that you're depriving your child if, for example, you hold him while he eats, carry him when you're out and play with him on the floor instead of using a high chair, stroller or bouncer seat. You are actually doing him a favor.

- Items that are usually only used for a few months include:

  BASSINET

  CRADLE

  BOUNCER SEAT (a soft, sling-like seat on a metal or plastic frame)

  SWING

  INFANT FEEDING SEAT/HARD BABY CARRIER (a structured seat that isn't a car seat)

  SOFT BABY CARRIER (such as a Snugli® or a backpack)

  BABY BATHTUB

  MOBILE

  PLAYPEN

  ATTACHABLE SEAT (a seat that attaches to the dining table for babies weighing less than twenty-five pounds)

  WALKER (either the newer, more stable kind or the older rolling version)

  Consider your lifestyle before purchasing these pieces of equipment. If you decide you want to use them, these might be good items to be borrowed or bought second-hand.

- Items that tend to be used frequently over a period of a few years include:

  STROLLER

  COMBINATION INFANT/TODDLER CAR SEAT

  ROCKING CHAIR or **GLIDER CHAIR**

  CHANGING TABLE

  CRIB

  TRAVEL BED (also called portable play yards)

BABY MONITORS

SAFETY GATES

Consider your lifestyle. It might be worthwhile to invest in items in this category.

- Following are some items that you don't have to have, but that will seem absolutely invaluable once you've used them. Most are available at baby supply stores, department stores, discount stores and through catalogs.

CRIB BIBS are small terry cloth or soft fabric pads that attach with Velcro around the crib slats and cover the sheet where your newborn baby lies his head. As they become dirty you can easily change them, keeping your baby's sheets fresh without having to remake the entire crib.

CRIB SHEETS WITH VELCRO TABS that connect to the slats of the crib are much easier to put on than regular fitted sheets. They take the trauma out of changing crib sheets.

> *I put a fitted crib sheet under a Velcro tab crib sheet on Trevor's crib. When the top sheet gets soiled, I just take it off. The clean fitted sheet is underneath ready to be used. That way, I have to change the crib half as often.* (Melissa)

A CUP HOLDER that attaches to the handle of your stroller is a great place to put your drink or the baby's bottle while you're pushing the stroller. These are particularly handy if they also have hooks on which to hang bags.

VELCRO TAB BOOTIES that close around the ankle are great. All other types of booties fall off quickly. These stay on a little longer before they fall off.

A BOUNCER SEAT with a comfortable, sling-like seat is a great place for your baby to relax and play, especially when you put a baby gym (a toy that has hanging toys for baby to swat at) over him. You can also use it as a feeding chair before your baby can sit in a high chair.

A RAIN GUARD that covers the entire stroller protects your baby if you live in a rainy climate.

If your baby uses a pacifier, a **PACIFIER LEASH** clips on to your baby's clothes to keep the pacifier clean and handy.

A **DIGITAL EAR THERMOMETER** takes the trauma out of taking your baby's temperature. You can even put it in his ear while he's sleeping. Within three seconds you'll know if he's sick. Adults can use it, too.

- Items that might tempt you, but that really aren't practical include:

A HIGH CHAIR WITH A RECLINING SEAT BACK: If your baby is too little to sit up straight, she's too little to need a high chair. You can use a bouncer seat, an infant seat, a swing (that's not moving, of course) or you can hold her in your lap when you feed her cereal.

A PLASTIC MAT that's designed to go under the car seat to protect the seat of your car: Some have notches for the seat belt; others don't. The ones that don't have notches have to be bunched up under the seat belt. Neither type protects the areas where babies really tend to make messes—on either side of the car seat. All the mats really do is protect the seat of your car from the base and the back of the car seat. A towel placed under the car seat is an economical and easy-to-clean alternative.

BIBS THAT SLIP OVER THE BABY'S HEAD: When you take them off, anything that's on the bib gets on baby's hair. Bibs that snap, Velcro or tie are an easier alternative. I specifically recommend bibs made of plastic (either the hard kind or the soft ones) since they can be wiped off with a diaper wipe or washed in the sink then dried with a towel. Keep the cute cloth bibs for catching drool and spit up, not food.

THE COMFORTER THAT MATCHES YOUR CRIB SET: These are extremely expensive and tend to be too bulky to actually use. Soft blankets are a more practical alternative.

Shopping Strategies

The key to successful shopping is deciding what's important to you before you go. Learn about all the features and consider how they'll affect your life with your baby. Prepare a prioritized list of the functions you want each piece of equipment to perform.

As you shop, your major considerations should be how well and how easily the item does what you want it to do. One criteria without the other isn't enough. If something works, but is difficult to use, you probably won't use it. If it's easy to use, but ineffective, there's no point having it. The best way to figure out whether an item meets these criteria is to test it out before you buy it. Open and close it, pick it up, try it out with a ten-pound bag of something in it. Then, once the item is yours, make sure to use it properly. If you have any questions or problems, contact the manufacturer. A list of manufacturer's phone numbers is provided in the Resource Guide in the back of the book.

- There are three major categories of criteria for selecting baby equipment: your convenience (which includes price and ease of use), your baby's comfort and your baby's safety. Think about the trade-offs when you look at baby equipment.

- *Consumer Reports Guide to Baby Products* is a helpful resource when evaluating specific brands and styles of baby equipment. It's available at bookstores and libraries. *Consumer Reports* magazine also evaluates particular brands and models of baby equipment. Ask a librarian to help you find the right issues or call Consumer's Union at 914-378-2740.

- When you're evaluating several brands or models of a certain piece of equipment, first compare them according to how well they meet your basic needs. Then look at all the extra features. It doesn't do you any good to have a stroller that looks great, for example, if it's difficult to fold up and get into your car.

- If you want assistance in selecting baby equipment, go to a specialty baby store. The sales staff at these stores are knowledgeable about the products and can help you find the appropriate items to meet your needs. Clerks at discount, toy and department stores generally know the product features, but often can't relate those features to actual use of the product.

> *My friend and I went shopping for baby equipment together. We laughed hysterically as we practically fell flat on our faces trying to open and close strollers. After numerous attempts, we still couldn't figure out how to lower the sides of cribs. As embarrassed as we were at our clumsiness, all that experimenting helped us figure out what features we liked and didn't like.* (Monique)

- If you're making your purchases at a baby store, comparison shop. Most stores will negotiate the price with you, especially if you're buying several large items at once. Delivery and set-up charges are easy items on which to save some money if you're uncomfortable negotiating price. Some stores will waive this fee if you've made a large purchase. Just ask them.

- If you will be setting up a piece of equipment, make sure to include ease of assembly in your list of features to consider when selecting your purchases.

  Jon and I spent a whole day buying and assembling baby equipment. The swing didn't seem too complicated, but we just couldn't get it to swing properly. We were just about to take it back to the store when we decided to call the manufacturer to make sure we weren't missing something. Sure enough there was a simple trick to make it work. It figures, I finally get my husband to read the instructions and crucial information is missing! (Karen)

- Save your receipts and packaging. Don't be afraid to exchange products that aren't working out for you. Only shop at stores which gladly accept exchanges or returns. You won't regret it.

- Send in every warranty or registration card that comes with the products you purchase. Not only will this assist you to get replacement parts or service if something breaks, but it allows the manufacturer to notify you if the product has been recalled.

- Consignment shops that sell used baby equipment are a wonderful way to get baby clothes and equipment inexpensively, especially those items that you will only be using for a few months. Consignment shops can be found in the yellow pages under "Clothing-Consignment and Used." Look for one that specializes in children's items. Many consignment stores also advertise in local parenting newspapers and magazines. Call them before you go to make sure they have the types of items you want.

- Consignment stores are also a great way to sell gifts you can't return, items you used but didn't like, or good quality maternity and baby clothes you don't plan to use again.

CHAPTER FOURTEEN

Selecting Baby Equipment

Once you've determined which pieces of baby equipment you need and what functions you want them to perform, use the following lists to help you determine which specific products, models and styles are the best for you. These lists are just a sample of the features to consider, however, since manufacturers seem to be redesigning their products all the time.

Review the lists and develop your own wish list of features before you go to the store. Then bring the list with you when you shop. This will dramatically reduce the time it takes to purchase what you need. It will also help you make careful decisions that maximize your baby's safety, your convenience and the value you get for your money. Once you've determined the best options based on these criteria and your budget, you can decide which one is the cutest or best matches your decor.

Items You Use at Home
CRIB

* If you're buying a **NEW CRIB**, you can be confident that it was made according to current safety guidelines. Style and ease of use can be your major concern. Consider:

  ❏ How easy is it to raise and lower the side of the crib? Remember, if you choose a crib that has a fold-down, rather than a slide-down side, you might need two hands to open or close it. This can be a difficult maneuver when you're holding a baby.

❑ Can both sides or only one side be lowered?

❑ Can the sides of the crib be removed to turn it into a toddler bed?

❑ How many mattress level adjustments are there?

❑ Does it have casters so you can easily move the crib? If so, can they be locked so the crib will only roll when you want it to?

• When you're considering a **USED CRIB**, you must also carefully evaluate its safety features:

❑ Is the space between the slats 2 3/8 inches or less, as it should be?

❑ Is there a minimum of nine inches between the lowered side of the crib and the mattress support when it's in its highest setting and a minimum of twenty-six inches when it's in its lowest setting, as there should be?

❑ Is the mattress rack sturdy enough? Test it by applying a lot of pressure to one side of the mattress. The other side of the mattress shouldn't come up.

❑ Does the mattress fit tightly into the crib with no spaces around the edges?

❑ Is the paint lead-free? Cribs made after 1978 should be okay. Ones from 1978 or before might not be. If you're not sure, test the paint (with a kit from a hardware or grocery store) or just go ahead and refinish the crib with safe paint.

❑ Are there any dangerous posts or decorative accents on which a baby could catch his head, arms or clothing? There should be rounded edges at the top of the crib.

• Be aware that mattresses are generally sold separately from the crib.

• Unless you plan on having many children or passing the mattress along to family or friends, you don't need an expensive, top-of-the-line mattress that's guaranteed to last for years and years. Generally, kids are out of the crib by the time they're about three years old.

- It's a good idea to flip the crib mattress from end to end and from side to side occasionally. You'll use the whole mattress instead of letting one particular area get all the wear and tear.

CHANGING TABLE

- Things to look for:

  ❏ Is the base open on all sides? A changing table with open shelves will be difficult to use as a dresser or storage unit for anything but toys once your baby starts crawling around and getting into things.

  ❏ If it's also a dresser, is it sturdy enough that it won't tip over if all the drawers are pulled out and an adventuresome toddler climbs on them? (Also note: any dresser you purchase should also meet this criteria.)

  ❏ Is the height of the table appropriate for you? You'll be spending a lot of time leaning over this piece of equipment.

- A changing pad that can be attached to a dresser makes an economical and practical changing table. Most pads attach by screwing tabs into the back of the dresser. Once your baby is too old for a changing table, simply remove the pad and continue to use the dresser.

DIAPER PAIL

- When you select an "odorless" diaper pail that wraps the diapers in plastic, be sure to consider how many steps are involved in putting the diaper into the diaper pail, how big the pail is and whether you need to purchase special bags or can use regular trash bags. From an environmental perspective, you might also want to think about how many layers of plastic are involved in this process.

- Diaper pail deodorizers are available in the baby section of most grocery stores. They really help. Unfortunately, they're also poisonous, so keep them and the diaper pail out of your baby's reach.

- If you use cloth diapers and have a diaper service, they will probably provide you with a diaper pail. Check before you buy one.

BABY SWING

- Before you invest in a baby swing, make sure your baby likes using one. First try one at a friend's house or at a store.

- Consider:

  ❏ Does the swing need to be wound up or is it battery operated?

  ❏ If it needs to be wound up, how long does it run after you wind it?

  ❏ How much noise does it make when you wind it up? This is an important consideration because it can be very frustrating to startle your baby awake when you wind the swing.

  ❏ Does it have a variable speed setting?

  ❏ Is the seat adjustable?

  ❏ Does it have a toy tray attachment?

  ❏ Is the padding removable and washable?

  ❏ Is there a cradle attachment?

  ❏ Can the seat be removed and used separately?

- Baby swings with a cradle attachment that swings from head to foot have been recalled for safety reasons. Only use a cradle attachment that swings from side to side.

HIGH CHAIR

- When you choose a high chair, consider what you'll want for your older infant or toddler, not a newborn. Lots of high chairs offer features specifically for newborns, but you really don't need a high chair until your baby is about six months old, when he can sit up and is ready for solid food. If he's eating before he sits up, you can hold him or put him in a baby seat with a reclined back.

- What to look for:

  ❏ Is there a tray or does it fit up against a table?

  ❏ Is the tray removable?

  ❏ Does the tray have antibacterial protection?

❏ How many tray positions are there? Notice how close the tray can be placed to the seat. The tray needs to fit close to your baby's body for safety and to stop food from falling in his lap.

❏ Do you need one or two hands to adjust the tray?

❏ How easy is it to adjust the tray?

❏ Is there a rim or a trough around the edge of tray to prevent spills from dripping over?

❏ Can the tray be put in the dishwasher?

❏ What is the depth between the tray and the seat? Too little space and your baby won't have room to move his legs, too much and the tray may be too high for a small baby.

❏ Does the seat back recline?

❏ Is it designed so there are few crevices where food and dirt could collect?

❏ How stable is the high chair?

❏ Is it foldable for easy storage?

❏ Does it adjust to different heights?

❏ Is it padded? If so, how sturdy is the padding?

❏ Is there a safety belt?

❏ Is there are bar or a strap that goes between baby's legs?

❏ How easy is it to attach the safety belt?

❏ Can the safety belt be removed and washed?

❏ Is the safety belt adjustable for use with an infant as well as a toddler?

❏ Does it convert into a booster seat for a toddler?

SAFETY GATE

- Consider:

  ❏ What are its maximum and minimum widths?

  ❏ Does it need to be hardware mounted or is it a pressure gate? Hardware mounted is safest for around stairs; a pressure gate is fine between rooms.

  ❏ How easy is it to open and close?

  ❏ How high is it? If you want to be able to step over it without opening and closing it, a lower gate would be better.

  ❏ Is there anything on the gate, either a bar or a large opening, that a toddler could climb on?

  ❏ If it's an older gate, does it have wide, open "V's" along the top? If so, the gate isn't safe to use.

- Pet stores often sell safety gates at lower prices than baby stores do. If you need to buy a safety gate to put in a standard-sized doorway, try a pet store first.

BABY MONITOR

- You will want to know:

  ❏ How far is the range it will cover?

  ❏ How many channels does it have?

  ❏ Are there sound indicator lights and/or video in addition to sound?

  ❏ Are there rechargeable batteries, regular batteries, and/or cords to plug in the receiver and monitor?

  ❏ Is there a low battery indicator?

  ❏ Is there a scrambling system to ensure your privacy?

- If your cordless phone has a lot of static after you turn on the baby monitor, experiment by changing the channels on the phone and on the monitor.

- You may have heard stories about people hearing their neighbors' baby crying or cordless phone conversations on the baby monitor. You can believe them! If this happens to you, try switching channels on the baby monitor. They might be hearing you, too.

- Be careful what you say in a room that has the recording part of the baby monitor. Remember that people in the room with the listening device can hear you.

Items You Use in the Car
INFANT CAR SEAT

- Things to look for:

  ❑ How much does it weigh? You'll be carrying this around a lot. A few pounds can make a huge difference.

  ❑ Does it have a five point or three point harness?

  ❑ How easy is it to adjust the harness?

  ❑ Does it fit into your car? The base must fit in your car's seat. The length of the seat from front to back must also fit between the front and back seats or between the front seat and the dash. In some smaller cars and cars with deep bucket seats, some rear-facing infant seats will only fit in the front seat. (Note: never put a rear-facing infant car seat in the front passenger seat of a car with an activated passenger-side air bag.)

  ❑ How easy is it to buckle the seat into the car?

  ❑ What type of carrying handles does it have? Put fifteen pounds of weight in and carry it around to see if it's comfortable and manageable.

  ❑ Does it have a removable base that stays in the car? This feature enables you to snap the seat into the base instead of buckling and unbuckling the seat belt each time you take the seat in and out of the car. If it does have a base, how easy is it to remove and replace the seat? Can the car seat be used without the base in case you want to use it in another car without moving the base?

  ❑ Is the padding removable and washable?

❑ Will it fit into your stroller? If it does, you won't have to wake your sleeping baby if you want to transfer him from the car to the stroller.

❑ Does it have a hood?

❑ Does it have compartments for toys, bottles, etc.?

❑ How easy is it to push the release button for the restraint strap? This is especially important if you plan on keeping any fingernails whatsoever or if you lack the finger strength of a master rock climber.

❑ Does it have a pull-out stand on the bottom so you can use it as either a stable seat or a rocking seat when you're using it outside of the car?

❑ Does it have latches to attach it to a shopping cart?

COMBINATION INFANT/TODDLER CAR SEAT

- *Consumer Reports* has found that it's safest to use an infant car seat, rather than a rear-facing convertible car seat, for an infant.

- While it might seem more economical to purchase just a combination infant/toddler seat, also called a convertible car seat, it's certainly not convenient for you or your baby. Since this type of seat is too large and bulky to hold or put in your stroller, you won't be able to carry your baby around in it. You'll have to hold him or transfer him to a stroller or infant seat. If you use an infant car seat, you don't have to disturb him by taking him out of the car seat. You can just carry him around in the car seat.

- According to *Consumer Reports'* evaluation of convertible car seats, the advantages and disadvantages of the various types of seats include:

  FIVE-POINT HARNESS: easy to buckle and unbuckle, but the straps can get in the way when you put the child into the seat.

  T-SHIELD: easy to buckle and unbuckle and to move the straps out of the way when you're going to place the child in the seat, but a small infant's head might not clear the shield.

  OVERHEAD SHIELD: easy to use and adjust the straps, but doesn't protect against head injury as well as other designs and a small infant's head might not clear the shield.

- New cars and front-facing car seats are required to have top tethers and anchors to ensure that car seats are installed properly and provide as much protection as possible. Even if you already have or can borrow an old car seat, the safety benefits of these new systems may make it worthwhile to buy one.

- If you want the safety benefits of a top tether but don't want to buy a new car seat and/or your car doesn't have an anchor for a top tether, you can modify your car seat and car. Kits are available for installing top tethers on car seats and anchors on cars. Contact your car seat manufacturer or car dealer.

- If you and your partner will be using different cars to pick up and drop off your baby at child care, it might be worthwhile to have one car seat for each car. The extra cost might be less of a problem than the hassles of taking the car seat out of one car, leaving it at the child care facility, installing it in the other car, then moving it back to the first car the next day. Even if you don't have to worry about taking turns going to the child care facility, it might be worth it to have two car seats. That way you don't always have to use the same car when you go out with your baby.

  We switched the car seat back and forth from car to car until the day my husband drove off with the car seat in his car. He had to come home from work to bring it back to me so I could take Layla to child care before I went to work. The money we lost by missing hours of work was far more than the expense of the new car seat we bought that night. (Zoe)

- When you look at combination infant/toddler car seats, consider:

  ❏ What size baby can safely use the seat?

  ❏ Does it have a top tether strap?

  ❏ How many reclining positions does it have?

  ❏ Are there special pads that offer additional head support for infants?

  ❏ What other type of padding does it have?

  ❏ Is the padding removable and washable?

❑ Does the base of the car seat fit in your car?

❑ How easy is it to buckle into your car? This is less important than with an infant seat because you probably won't be moving this seat in and out of the car as often.

❑ Does it have a five-point or three-point harness? Does it have a belt restraint only, a T-shield or an overhead shield (a tray-like shield that swings down over baby's head and is positioned in front of him when the buckle is latched)? Buckling up a five-point system typically requires two or three steps: first putting the baby's arms through the straps, then buckling the upper straps into the strap between the legs. A three-point system requires that you pull the straps, and the bar if there is one, down over baby's head them snap the single buckle. In each of these designs, you also need to position the safety clip on the straps after buckling the baby into the car seat.

❑ Where is the release button and how easy is it to push? Would a clever and determined toddler be able to get herself out of the car seat if she wanted to?

COMBINATION STROLLER/CAR SEAT

• Things to think about:

❑ If you buy a combination stroller/car seat that consists of an infant car seat and a stroller attachment that holds the car seat now and turns into a toddler stroller later, you've truly purchased three pieces of equipment in one. You can continue to use the stroller even after the baby is out of the infant car seat.

❑ If you buy a car seat and a stroller attachment that's basically a rolling stand for the car seat, you'll still have to get a stroller when your baby outgrows the infant car seat.

❑ The biggest disadvantage of a car seat/stroller combination is that your baby never gets a chance to change position. You don't have the option of laying him down to sleep in the stroller. You might also find that your baby gets fussy in the car more often since he's sitting in his car seat for longer periods of time.

❑ The car seat/stroller might be perfect for your situation (if you get around the city by taxi, for example), but be sure you consider all the ramifications of your decision. You're definitely prioritizing your convenience over your baby's comfort.

❑ If you decide to use a combination stroller/car seat, use the factors to consider when selecting a stroller (listed below) and a car seat (listed previously) to evaluate both aspects of the product.

Items You Use When You're Out With Your Baby
STROLLER

* Consider:

  ❑ How easy is it to pick up and move? Weight alone isn't relevant. Pick up the stroller and test how easy it will be to take it in and out of your trunk or on and off a bus. A few pounds more might not make a difference if the stroller is better balanced and designed.

  ❑ How big is it when it's closed? Does it fit in your trunk, your garage, your storage area?

  ❑ How does it open and close? How many steps are there to opening it? Do you push or pull something on the handle or push a bar with your foot? Does it take one or two steps to fold it up? One step might be more convenient for you, but having two steps helps ensure that it won't accidentally fold up with your baby in it.

  ❑ Does it have a locking mechanism that keeps it from unfolding when it's meant to be closed?

  ❑ Does it stand up by itself when it's closed? This makes it easier to store when you put it in your garage or take it to a restaurant or other public place.

  ❑ Does it have single or double wheels? Double wheels make it more stable and easier to steer.

  ❑ Is the handle reversible? A reversible handle can be positioned so you can steer the stroller and look directly at your newborn, then reverse the handles so an older baby can look forward.

❏ Are the handles at a level that's comfortable for both you and your partner?

❏ Is (are) the handle(s) adjustable?

❏ How adjustable is the seat back? Does it lay flat? How many reclining levels are there?

❏ Are there brake locks on two or four wheels?

❏ Is there a five-point harness, a three-point harness (a belt around baby's waist and through his legs) or just a safety belt?

❏ How easy is it to buckle and unbuckle the safety belt? Belts with buckles are much easier than belts that have to be threaded through rings. Some buckles are easier to unfasten than others. Test them out.

❏ Is the padding removable and washable?

❏ How thick is the padding?

❏ Does it have a hood?

❏ Is there a plastic window in the hood so you can view your baby while you stroll?

❏ Does it have a basket? If so, how big is it?

❏ Is there a footrest?

❏ Is the footrest adjustable?

❏ Is there a bar or tray in front of the seat?

❏ Does it have shock absorbers? (Don't laugh, some do.)

❏ Does it have a removable cover that goes over the baby's legs?

I always wondered why I saw moms in malls carrying their babies as they pushed the stroller full of bags. Now I know. It's hard to push a stroller while you're carrying a lot of stuff. If your basket is too small and you don't have any way to hook the shopping bags onto the stroller handle, the easiest solution is to put your purchases in the stroller. (Olivia)

- If walking or jogging is your form of regular exercise, it might be worthwhile to invest in a "baby jogger" type stroller. These three-wheeled strollers are built to take the punishment of the streets. Standard strollers might not be able to stand up to the stress. The jogger stroller also rolls faster, has higher handles so you don't have to bend over to push and requires less effort to push. They are, however, much more difficult to maneuver through restaurant and store aisles. You might want to have a standard-type stroller to use when you're not walking or jogging.

- A lot of mothers find that fold-up umbrella-type strollers are easier to use than standard strollers. They're certainly a lot less expensive. They also fit into cars and airplanes better, are easier to pick up and are more maneuverable in tight places. They're not the best option for a newborn, but if you don't plan on using the stroller until your baby is older, you might not need a standard stroller with all the bells and whistles at all.

DIAPER BAG

- You don't have to use a diaper bag for a diaper bag. Any big bag will do.

- Diaper bags with shorter double shoulder straps tend to stay put better than ones with one long strap. Bags with double straps can easily be held back with your elbow. Bags with a long single strap tend to swing forward or fall off when you bend down to pick up the baby or open the stroller. Be sure to move around with the diaper bag straps on your shoulder to see if the bag stays in place.

- A lot of new parents find that a backpack, whether it's designed to be a diaper bag or not, is a convenient alternative to the traditional diaper bag. The double straps take the pressure off your shoulders, they fit easily over the handles of many strollers and they tend to be very sturdy. In addition, when you bend down to pick up your baby, a backpack stays in place.

- Washable changing pads can be bought separately from the diaper bag if you need a new one or an extra one. A cost-free option is to just use a towel.

- Things to look for:

  ❑ What are the size and location of pockets and compartments?

  ❑ Does it have an insulated compartment for bottles and food? If so, is it conveniently located?

  ❑ Is there a compartment for your keys, money, etc.?

  ❑ Is the bag big enough to carry everything you need for an entire day or just a few essentials?

  ❑ Is there a plastic bag for dirty clothes? If so, is it removable and washable?

  ❑ Is there a removable changing pad? Changing pads that are attached to the diaper bag can be inconvenient when your baby is longer or old enough to try to get into the diaper bag while you're changing him.

  ❑ Are the straps adjustable or do they fit you and your partner as they are?

  ❑ Are the straps long enough to fit over the handle of your stroller so you can hang the diaper bag instead of holding it?

  ❑ Are the straps long enough that you can put them over your shoulder, or do you need to carry the bag in your hand?

  ❑ Does the bag fit in the basket of your stroller?

  ❑ What style bag is it? Does it look like a piece of soft luggage, a baby bag or a classy purse?

  ❑ Does it close with a zipper, Velcro or snaps?

  ❑ Can it be machine washed or just wiped with a cloth?

I was really excited to find a gorgeous black, leather-looking diaper bag with gold chain shoulder straps. My husband Donald liked it when I held it, but then he realized it would look like he was carrying a purse when he used it. Needless to say, we ended up with a backpack-style diaper bag that we both felt comfortable with. (Pat)

SOFT BABY CARRIER

- Many of the factors to consider when selecting a soft baby carrier also apply when you're shopping for a backpack type carrier.

- I strongly recommend that you test out any baby carrier before you purchase or borrow it. They vary widely in comfort, features and convenience. When you test one, test it with a ten pound load, a fifteen pound load, a twenty pound load, etc. What was comfortable with ten pounds might be painful with twenty.

- Unless your soft baby carrier or backpack comes with a special, built-in stand so it can be used as a free-standing baby seat, don't use it as one.

- Evaluate:

  ❏ What size baby can safely use the carrier?

  ❏ Does the baby face front and/or back?

  ❏ Is the seat adjustable to fit your baby as he grows?

  ❏ Is it sturdy enough to support your baby without you holding on to him?

  ❏ Does it have a removable, washable cloth where the baby's face or head rests?

  ❏ Does it completely cover the baby up or is it more open?

  ❏ Does the baby's weight rest on your back, shoulders, hip or stomach?

  ❏ Are the shoulder straps padded?

  ❏ Is there a safety belt for the baby?

  ❏ How complicated is it to put on and take off?

❏ Can you put it on and take it off by yourself?

❏ Is it proportioned to suit both you and your partner?

❏ Is it easily adjustable? This is important, for example, so that you can wear it over your coat outside, then adjust it to fit you when you've gone inside and taken your coat off.

❏ Is there a storage area for items such as a diaper, pacifier or toy?

PORTABLE PLAY YARD/TRAVEL BED

- It's good to have a portable play yard if you want your baby to take naps or sleep when you're away from home. They're great for taking to friends' houses, for example, if your baby doesn't like to nap in her car seat or stroller or on a blanket. If your baby frequently sleeps over at a relative's house, a portable play yard can be a low cost and space saving alternative to a crib. On the other hand, if the only time your baby sleeps away from home is at a hotel or a home with a crib, you probably don't need one.

    The travel bed became one of my most used pieces of baby equipment. I kept it downstairs in the family room when Alexandra was an infant. Having it there for naps and quiet play time saved me from running upstairs to her room all the time. Now I keep it in the trunk of my car. When we visit friends, its a safe, familiar place for her to play and rest. (Mamie)

- Things to think about:

    ❏ How much does it weigh?

    ❏ What size (height and weight) baby can use it?

    ❏ How easy is it to assemble?

    ❏ How easy is it to disassemble?

    ❏ What size is it when it's set up? A bigger one might be better if you plan to use it frequently at home or at the office. A smaller one might be better if you plan to use it frequently in hotel rooms.

❏ Does it have a bassinet feature for use with young infants who cannot yet get up on their hands and knees?

❏ Does it have a changing table feature?

❏ Is there a pocket for toys?

❏ Is there a canopy? This is a handy feature if you plan to use the play yard outside.

❏ Is there a storage bag you can keep it in when it's not being used?

❏ Can it vibrate?

❏ Does it have wheels so you can move it around easily?

❏ Is there a removable, washable sheet?

Section Six

Managing Family Dynamics

Having a baby not only changes how you think of yourself, but also how others in your immediate and extended family think of you and interact with you. The adjustments can be a bit bumpy at times, even in the best of relationships. In situations with blended families or divorced grandparents, things can be even more complicated.

I guarantee that it's worth it for you, the baby and everyone else to get off to a good start as you all adapt to these new relationships. As with most other aspects of motherhood, it's generally easier to establish good patterns now than to break bad ones later. Remember, you won't only affect your own interaction with your family. You'll also improve the quality of the family environment in which your child will grow up.

CHAPTER FIFTEEN

You, Your Partner and Your Baby

Adjusting to Being Parents

A new set of dynamics is created when a couple has a baby. If you've read the previous chapters, I've probably already convinced you that a whole new definition for "normal" needs to be created after a baby joins your family. (If you haven't read that part, just trust me on this!) Your partner, however, no matter how thrilled he is to have the baby, may still be waiting for the old version of normal to reappear. You might need to help him make his expectations of you and your shared lifestyle more appropriate so the transition from couple to family will be a smooth one.

Working together to define positive patterns for sharing the responsibility of baby care will help you both adjust more quickly and easily to parenthood. Together you can create a supportive, satisfying sense of life balance for both of you. Oh, and while you're working on this, don't forget that you still have a relationship as partners, not just as parents.

- Remember that you were not the only one who experienced the birth of your baby. Your partner was part of it, too. It was probably a momentous event for him, but few people will ask for his perspective on labor and delivery. Encourage him to talk about the birth and to share his joy, excitement and pride.

- Your partner might have thanked you for making him a father. He might even have given you a gift or flowers to celebrate your motherhood. Don't forget to thank him for helping you during labor and delivery and to celebrate his new role as a father.

- If you've been home with the baby, try not to treat your partner as the relief shift the minute he returns from work. He might need some time to unwind before he's ready to take care of the baby.

- If your partner works while you're with the baby, he might tend to think that since the baby is with you all day, it's his turn to be with you in the evening. While you should be able to take some of your attention away from the baby, remind your partner that your job as a mother continues around the clock. It doesn't just stop because the workday is over. Remind him that his expectations of your time and attention need to adapt to the new reality.

- You may find that once the baby is in bed for the night, you feel like you finally have some time to yourself. Unfortunately, this is also the time that your partner has been anticipating spending with you. Explain your need for some time alone. With an understanding partner, you can probably work out an evening pattern that's comfortable for both of you.

- Some dads act as if they need to be assigned a specific baby-care responsibility before they do anything. If your partner acts like this, gently remind him that he is a parent, not a helper.

- Remind your partner that his schedule and priorities need to adjust to the new family structure, too. He can't just help you when it's convenient for him. He shares the responsibility for caring for the baby.

It drives me crazy that when my husband wants to go out alone in the evening, he just checks to see whether any other activities are planned for that night. When I want to go out, he acts like it's a big deal that he's "baby-sitting." How come it's just assumed that I'll stay with the baby when he goes out, but when I want to go out I have to make special arrangements with him? (Kathy)

My husband and I have a deal. If one of us goes out at night, we aren't expected to come back before Kynsi is put to bed. In fact, the longer we stay out the better. This helps us avoid feeling guilty for not rushing back, makes the time we spend away more relaxed and gives the other person some quiet time alone in the house. (Marcia)

- Dad should be able to identify the baby's needs and act without prompting from you. Some men have explained to me that they don't notice the baby's needs until the mother points them out because they, as men, only focus on one thing at a time. According to them, it's not that they are ignoring the baby's needs—it's that they truly don't notice. I don't consider this a valid excuse. Neither should you. Mothers have to develop the skill of being aware of the baby while they focus on other things. Fathers should be able to develop this skill, also.

  My husband thinks that if he's going to be left alone with the baby, baby care is all he can be doing during that time. Consequently, he expects me to give him time to shower, read the mail, make phone calls and do everything he might possibly do for himself before I leave. He forgets that I'm supposed to be able to do all those things while I'm with the baby. Why can't he? Now I'm purposely trying to leave at times when he has to take care of Michaela at the same time he does other things. He needs the practice. He also needs to gain some respect for what I do every day. (Jessica)

- If you both work, experiment with the before and after work schedule. Figure out something that's best for both of you, then try to stick to it at least for a while. Don't make too many changes or a time could come, for example, when each of you thinks that the other one is picking up the baby from child care.

- When you're home during the day with the baby, it's normal for you to be the one to handle many household chores. You may even be comfortable doing some of the chores your partner usually does. But unless you come to a mutual agreement that you are responsible for everything in the house, your partner shouldn't get to avoid all of his household responsibilities just because he's earning an income and you're not. You're definitely doing an important, challenging and time consuming "job."

- It's not unusual for new fathers to have difficulty adjusting to nighttime feedings and to want to sleep in another room. This is purely a matter between you and your partner. Tell him if you're not happy with the idea. Some women, on the other hand, actually like it—they don't have to try so hard to be quiet.

- Relax when your partner is taking care of or playing with the baby. Allow father and child to develop their own relationship and routines. He might do things differently than you do, but too much criticism might result in him not wanting to take care of the baby at all.

- It can be tempting to trade off taking care of the baby. While your partner is doing something else, you care for the baby. When you need time to do something, he'll take care of the baby. Make sure you spend time taking care of the baby together, too. Not only does this make caring for the baby easier, it also gives you an opportunity to have family time.

- Encourage your partner to venture out with the baby as soon as possible. The longer he puts off taking the baby out by himself, the harder it might be to overcome any nervousness he's feeling.

- Talk about how parenthood is affecting your partner's and your own emotions, responsibilities at home, responsibilities at work, sense of life balance, hopes and dreams. You can be more supportive of each other when you understand the other's point of view. It will also help you create a new lifestyle that works for your unique situation and preferences.

    Mike and I found plenty of time to discuss ways to solve existing problems and to troubleshoot potential ones. We finally realized that we should also spend some time talking more pro-actively. We needed to discuss how we ideally wanted things to be as we changed our busy lives in order to spend more time with Hannah. Then we could figure out how to make that happen. The number of problems decreased and we both felt more in control. (Marlene)

- Continue to nurture your partnership as you adjust to your relationship as parents. Find ways to continue a relationship that is independent of your baby. The tips in Section Eleven on finding and using baby-sitters can help you accomplish this goal.

- Don't leave opportunities to be alone together to chance. Schedule "dates" with your partner. Get a baby-sitter, have a romantic dinner after the baby is in bed for the night, agree not to do anything but be together at a certain time, and/or do whatever it takes to make time to focus on each other. You might even want to set regular times to relax together, such as during the baby's Saturday afternoon nap or Friday night after the baby's in bed. You can also schedule a baby-sitter on a regular basis so you can count on having time alone, away from the baby.

Your Sex Life

Sex is an important part of maintaining your relationship with your partner. Although it's a reality that motherhood affects the sexual side of your relationship, which in turn affects the rest of your interaction, this can be a romantic, sexy time if you let it.

- During the first post-partum months, be sensitive to your partner's sexual needs. Your partner respected your physical needs throughout your pregnancy and post-partum recovery. Now he's probably anxious to re-establish the physical side of your relationship.

- Explain to your partner how pregnancy and childbirth have affected your body. After having a baby suck at your breast, tug on your hair, lie in your arms or hold your hand almost all day long, you might not be in the mood for your partner's touch at night. You might just want to be left alone to sleep. This is a common feeling among new mothers, but not something partners are likely to consider.

- When you're not in the mood, be sure to remind your partner that it has nothing to do with your feelings for him. It has to do with how you feel about yourself, your body and your new role, not to mention your exhaustion.

> *Kenny and I had always laughed at the stories of parents not being able to have sex because they were always being interrupted by the baby crying. We sort of thought it was one of those TV and movie stereotypical situations. Then Tyler was born. We realized that we heard about it so much because it happens so much! Once the baby cries, it's really hard to get back in the mood!* (Katie)

- Strive for quality, not quantity, of sex. The demands of life with a new baby do affect the sexual activity level of many new parents!

- When you're frazzled from the never-ending responsibilities of motherhood and feel that sex is that last thing you want, ask yourself whether fooling around with your partner might be just what you need to reduce your stress and relieve your tension. It may be hard to quickly shift gears from being maternal to being sexy, but you might find that once you start, it's nice to feel and act like your old self again.

- Now that you're a mother, the type of foreplay that excites you might have changed. Suddenly, your breasts are not just for sexual activities; they're also for feeding your child. You've just given birth and your vagina might be more used to discomfort than pleasure. In fact, after everything you've been through, you might like to just forget these body parts for a while. Don't worry, these are common feelings. While your foreplay preferences might change for a while, look at this as a time to experiment and find new ways to be sensual and sexual.

- If you wish you could get in the mood for sex, but you're too tired at night when you finally get in bed, remember that sex doesn't have to be reserved for nighttime. There's nothing wrong with being romantic in the afternoon while the baby is napping!

  I was so tired that I when I finally got to bed at night, I wanted to go to sleep as quickly as possible! When Mark was in the mood for sex, I knew that he was expressing his love for me, but I still felt like he was being insensitive to my intense need for sleep. We finally found that the best time for fooling around was in the morning, after Jason had been fed and was asleep or playing in his crib. At that point, I felt like my day had already started, so it was a treat to stay in bed a little longer even if I wasn't sleeping. (Ariana)

CHAPTER SIXTEEN

You, Your Baby and Your Other Child

If your new baby already has a sibling, it's just as important to maintain your relationship with your older child as it is to develop a good one with the new baby. Juggling everything you have to do is an ongoing, often exhausting reality of life. Just remember that your feelings are just as important as theirs. Respecting each person's individuality will help all of you adjust.

- It's normal and natural to feel more "in love" with one or another of your children at any given point in time. Don't feel guilty if you feel totally enamored of your new baby. You don't love your other child any less, you're just being overwhelmed with the emotions about your new baby.

- Allow your older child to welcome the baby into the family. Help her hold him, no matter how young she is.

- When you talk about the baby, call him "our" baby or "your" sister/brother. Encourage your older child to feel loving and possessive of the baby.

- If you can't pick up your older child while you're recovering from childbirth, tell him it's because your body hurts, not because he's too heavy. This will help him avoid feeling as if he's done something wrong.

- Although you'll be spending a lot more time taking care of children, don't forget to take time for yourself. Involve your older child in entertaining the baby or listening for him to wake from his nap so you can get a few minutes to take care of yourself.

    Brandon is at the age when he wants to have more trust and responsibility, so I ask him to "baby-sit" Justin while I'm busy doing housework or exercising upstairs. I make sure it's at a time when the baby has just been fed and changed and is in a playful mood. I give Brandon suggestions of how to play with Justin and pay him a dime. Not only does he seem thrilled that I recognize that he's a big boy, but he also seems to play more with the baby at other times. (Leslie)

- Don't tell your older child, "Don't worry, Mommy still loves you." The thought that you might not probably never occurred to her. Frequently tell her you love her and demonstrate your love through your actions. She will be reassured of your continued affection.

- Make a fuss over the new role of your older child. Tell visitors that he is now the big brother. Point out the differences in what he can do or have, such as snacks or TV, that the baby can't. This will help reinforce his desire to be a big kid versus a baby. Hopefully he won't want to regress to wearing diapers, nursing or drinking from bottles.

- If your older child does want to nurse or use a bottle, it's up to you whether or not to let her. If you're comfortable with the idea, she'll probably give it up soon after trying it. If you don't want her to try, offer her an attractive alternative, such as a special drink. Remind her that the baby can only have milk while she has a wide assortment of wonderful things that she can eat and drink.

- Many mothers feel somewhat guilty that they can now give less time to their older child. Rather than focus on how much time you can give him, make the most out of the time you do have with him.

- While you may have a million things to get done while your baby naps, use some of that time as special alone time with your older child. Additionally or alternately, make an effort to take your older child out for special times without the baby.

- If you find yourself continually telling your older child to wait until you're finished taking care of the baby before you help her, occasionally do the same to the baby. When he's fussy, tell him to wait while you take care of the other child. Your baby won't understand, but your older child will recognize the fairness of your actions once you point it out to her in this way.

- There's no sense feeling guilty about almost always making one child or another wait for your full attention. It is a fact of life when you have more than child. When you're busy taking care of the baby and your older child needs you, give him as much attention as possible while you're doing what you have to do. For example, encourage him to talk with you about what he needs even if you can't get up to help him. Some attention is better than none.

- Try to be realistic about what you tell an older child about when you can help her. Whenever possible, tie it to the completion of another activity rather than to a random time period. For example, say, "as soon as the baby is done nursing" rather than, "just a minute." Otherwise, your older child may think that a minute is half an hour long. This also may help her gauge the time herself, rather than having to repeatedly ask when you'll be ready.

- Some mothers say that when you have a second baby, the workload more than doubles. When you have a third or additional baby, the change is much less dramatic. Conventional wisdom aside, you'll just have to decide for yourself. Just know that you're not imagining a significant change in how much you have to do. You aren't just spending time taking care of the kids, you're also spending a lot of time and energy figuring how to juggle everything you have to do for each child.

- Don't be shocked to find that time passes differently when your new baby isn't your first baby. Last time, you didn't have a long-term perspective on baby care. You didn't know how long certain stages would last so they seemed to go on for a long time. This time, you know how long each stage tends to last. Some may seem to come and go so quickly you hardly have time to get used to them before they're gone.

- You may be pleasantly surprised to find that having another baby doesn't change your lifestyle as much as the first baby did. You're already used to planning your activities around a child's schedule, carrying lots of baby supplies and going to family-style places. You don't have to get used to that dramatic a change unless your older child has been out of the baby stage for a long time. Finally, something that's easier with more than one child!

- It may seem totally natural for you to focus on caring for the new baby and your partner to care for the older child. This is a necessity when you're busy nursing the baby, but it can damage family dynamics if it continues all the time. Your older child will miss you. Your partner won't be able to develop a strong relationship with the new baby. Try to trade off who takes care of whom and to have times when you are both taking care of a child together.

- Try to avoid comparing everything your baby does with what his older sibling did. This baby's personality and physical skills may be totally different. Look for his unique patterns and preferences. Remember to try things with him that didn't necessarily work with your other child. Just because your older child didn't like peas, for example, doesn't mean that this baby won't.

Timothy didn't like to chew food. He preferred smooth-textured baby food until he was a toddler. It didn't occur to me that Robin might have different tastes. I just bought the same types of baby food I was used to buying. It didn't even occur to me to do it any other way until a friend invited us to stay over for lunch and gave me a jar of baby food for Robin. She loved the chunky texture. I felt horrible, like I had been depriving my baby, but now I'm starting from scratch and offering her a much bigger variety of foods until I figure out what she likes best.
(Liz)

CHAPTER SEVENTEEN

You, Your Baby and the New Grandparents

Things were different when our parents were raising us. Less was known about car safety, recommendations for feeding babies were different and strollers, infant seats and other baby gadgets weren't as fancy or functional. While grandparents want to do what's best, they might not understand how to care for modern babies or mothers. If you don't communicate with the new grandparents about what you want and need, they won't know.

Hopefully, they'll welcome and respect your wishes. If they don't, you'll have to help them adjust to their role as grandparents. As hard as it might be, they have to get used to you being a parent, too. You'll need to stand firm and make it clear that you are the mother. You make the rules for your baby. You decide how things will be done for him.

Then, as your parents and in-laws learn to respect what you have to say, be sure to listen to them, too. Regardless of the tone in which it was offered, grandparents often do have good advice.

- Be honest and firm about your desire for visitors, including grandparents, during the first days or weeks. Whether you desperately want help or crave time alone with the baby, communicate your desires.

  When I was pregnant with my first baby, I told my mother that I wanted a few days to get used to the baby before she came. As soon as I went into labor three weeks early, however, I changed my mind. I called before I even left for the hospital and asked her to come. She left her house a few hours later and drove six hours to get to me. During the three weeks she stayed, she was totally supportive and gave me many helpful hints. Best of all, she knew just when I was ready for her to leave and did so gracefully. (Judith)

- Be clear about your rules and expectations of the new grandparents. For example, you may decide that it's okay for grandma to call and say she wants to come by in an hour or so, but not for her to just drop by unannounced. If you don't tell grandparents what the rules are, it will be hard to follow them.

- If you have a great relationship with your partner's parents, you may be able to communicate with them directly about your hopes for and expectations of them as grandparents. If not, your partner has a responsibility to talk with them. Don't just hope that he'll figure that out, though. The two of you should discuss how he'll handle general grandparent issues as well as specific problems.

- It's important to be aware of the most common misconceptions new grandparents often have so you can help them overcome them. Some of the outdated ideas include: The baby will get spoiled if you respond each time he cries. The baby needs to be covered with layers of clothes at all times. Babies can suffocate or choke on their vomit if they lie on their backs. Babies should be on a strict and regular feeding schedule. Mixing cereal into a newborn's milk or giving him cereal by spoon will help him sleep better. Babies can be given cereal as early as two weeks. Babies can catch a cold by being in a draft.

- Rules to Remind Grandparents:

  ❑ Respond to the baby whenever she cries. Remind them that this doesn't mean they have to pick her up or feed her each time. A reassuring voice, a pat on the back or help in reaching a toy may be the appropriate response for the situation.

  ❑ Newborns should be fed on demand, not on a schedule.

  ❑ The baby should be placed on his side or back to sleep until he's old enough to roll over and choose his own position.

❑ The baby must always be in the car seat in the car. If she needs to be taken out of the car seat, stop the car.

❑ The car seat cannot be in the front seat of a car with a passenger-side airbag.

❑ Don't give the baby any food that you haven't explicitly approved.

❑ Never pat a choking baby on the back. If the baby is coughing or crying, don't do anything. If the baby isn't making sounds and isn't breathing, do the Heimlich Maneuver.

❑ The baby's parents get to make the rules.

- Be firm and clear when you talk about your decisions, rules and ways of doing things. If you don't want to encourage grandparents to offer their opinions and suggestions, don't leave any room for negotiation.

- If grandparents still offer advice, that's okay, but make it clear that they don't get a vote. If they don't like how you handle things, acknowledge their comments, then tell them that you've made the choices that work best for your family. You certainly don't need to apologize for doing things differently than they would like.

- Don't feel guilty for doing things your way instead of your parents' way. You're not obligated to solicit their input or explain your decisions. You have every right to make choices that are appropriate for your situation and personal preferences, even if your parents aren't happy about it.

- Unless you have extremely strong feelings about what you want your children to call their grandparents, ask for the grandparents' suggestions. This can go a long way toward forming strong relationship—not just between your baby and his grandparents, but also between you, in your new role as a parent, and your parents or in-laws.

- Tell the grandparents about the baby's habits, preferences and signals. The more they understand him, the better they can care for him and interact with him.

- Remind grandparents how far babies can reach and how fast they can move. Breakable objects, jewelry, medicines and other dangerous items should be removed before your baby comes to their house.

- Be explicit in your directions. Tell them exactly what to do and how to do it.

  When David was seven months old, Grandma Gertye came to care for him for a day. I told her to give him juice in a cup, which he could hold himself. I showed her where the cup drawer was. I didn't tell her that she needed to put a lid on the cup. I guess I thought that was obvious since the lids were right there with the cups. She explicitly followed every direction I gave and gave him juice in a cup—without a lid. He, of course, dumped it all over himself. (Samantha)

- If grandparents aren't with your baby on a regular basis, remind them of the rules and "how to's" every time. Grandparents often don't remember how quickly babies change and grow.

- Anyone (including you) caring for your baby while she's eating should know the appropriate way to perform the Heimlich Maneuver on an infant. Courses are available at local recreation centers, YMCA's and hospitals.

- Remind grandparents that diapers are different than when you were a baby. They don't need to be changed every hour or two. On the flip side, disposable diapers and diaper covers for cloth diapers are so good these days that you can't always tell when a baby is wet or dirty. Just tell them how often to check whether the diaper needs to be changed.

- Think how you would feel if your child rebuffed all your efforts to provide comfort, love and assistance at an important time in his life. That's how your parents will feel if you don't let them take care of their child—you. Relax and enjoy the fact that someone wants to help you.

- When grandparents, or anyone for that matter, offer to help, accept it graciously. They're probably more than happy to do some of the things that you have to do all too often. Let them change diapers, spoon feed, put clothes on, etc. What's tedious to you might be fun to them. They won't be insulted that you asked them to do something helpful.

- If grandparents get overbearing, examine their motivation. Most likely, they're well-intentioned, but overly involved. Thank them for their advice, tell them you'll consider it, don't make any promises you don't intend to keep, then do what you feel is best.

- If grandparents seem to lack interest or to hold back their emotions or advice, it might be because they don't want to seem interfering or overbearing. To solve the problem, initiate a conversation about the role you're hoping they'll take with their grandchild. Be explicit about your desire for their involvement. It might pave the way for them to reach out to you and the baby in a way that's comfortable for everyone.

- Give grandparents some slack. They'll probably do things differently than you do, whether they mean to or not. Even if they bend the rules a little bit and give your three month-old a taste of ice cream or let your five month-old fall asleep with the bottle, not only will he survive, but he'll probably have little trouble getting back to the regular routine with you.

- When necessary, use your doctor as a scapegoat. Say, "I asked my doctor and he said that this is okay," or, "The doctor said to do it this way." How can anyone argue with that? (Although a grandparent might suggest you find another doctor.)

- Ask grandparents about their desire and ability to baby-sit. Don't just assume that they want to or are able to. Discuss the situations in which they will or won't baby-sit. Respect their decisions and preferences.

- If grandparents don't feel comfortable taking care of the baby on their own, it doesn't mean that they don't love you or your baby. Try to find other ways that they can help you and be involved in caring for him.

- Your baby's health and welfare are more important than grandparents' desires to baby-sit. If they aren't able to safely take care of your baby, don't leave her unsupervised with them. Find other ways they can help you take care of their grandchild. For example, they can push her in the stroller in the mall while you run into a store, sit in the back seat to play with her while you're driving and put her to bed at night while you do other things around the house.

- If grandparents want to be with you and your baby more often than you want, encourage them to make plans in advance with you. Set clear guidelines and communicate what you want. Encourage them to let you know what they want. That way, you'll all know what to expect.

CHAPTER EIGHTEEN

Dealing with Sensitive Family Dynamics

In many cases, dealing with step-families, divorced family members, in-laws and half-siblings is no different than dealing with any other family members. In some families, however, these relationships can be complicated. If this is your situation, the last thing you need as a new mother is another potential source of stress.

It's worth investing the emotional energy it takes to improve the interaction among extended family. There are many more family occasions that they'll be involved in now that you have a baby. If you start off on the right foot, you'll avoid a lot of problems, now and in the future.

- Welcoming a new baby into the world is a wonderful way to break down old barriers and form new relationships with relatives. For example, if you encourage your step-parent to have a strong relationship as your child's grandparent, you may actually end up strengthening the relationship between the two of you.

- Be sure to evaluate your own stress level over bringing together parents or other family members who are divorced or just don't get along. They might surprise you by ignoring each other and focusing on the baby. Don't worry too much until there's a reason to.

   I was very nervous about bringing the various factions of my extended family together at Melina's christening. At first I was more focused on making sure that all my family members were okay than I was on the baby or the ceremony. After I while I realized that the people who got along with each other were grouped into clumps, but that, for once, no one was arguing. (Molly)

- Important occasions such as hospital visits to see the new baby and the christening, bris, or baptism can bring together divorced or estranged family members who prefer not to see each other. Unless you're willing to have duplicate events so different people can attend at separate times, take responsibility for helping your relatives focus on the baby instead of each other. Remind them that you don't want your baby to be caught in the middle of family problems. Encourage them to leave their discomfort or hostilities at the door.

- Don't leave family members wondering about who will be at an event. They will probably be less stressed and more prepared to see people who make them uncomfortable if you tell them up front what to expect.

- Ask family members what they prefer to be called by your baby. If you have definite ideas about how formal or informal you want their titles to be, offer suggestions. Of course, once your baby starts to talk, they might end up with different nicknames altogether.

- Be sure to share important information and special mementos with all the various parts of your extended family. That way, no one's feelings get hurt because they didn't know when your baby got his first hair cut or learned to sit up, but someone else did. It's easier to make a few extra phone calls or photo reprints than to soothe someone's hurt feelings later.

- You don't need to worry about the quality of the relationship between your baby and a "real" relative versus that with a "step" relative. The more people who love and care for your child the better. If your direct relatives have a problem with your baby being close to a step-relative or an in-law, remind them of that fact and encourage them to develop strong relationships with your baby, too.

- It's tempting to try to make everything equal and fair among extended family members. It's seems appropriate, for example, to try to give your divorced parents equal amounts of time and the same opportunities to share special moments with you and your baby, but sometimes that just can't happen without using a computer program to generate a schedule. Just do the best you can do, so over time your family members have somewhat similar experiences.

- Different people have different relationships. You can't dictate how a relationship will develop. Just because you don't get along with someone doesn't mean that your baby won't! You may have to adapt your relationship with people out of respect for the relationships your baby develops.

- Having a baby may change the nature of your relationships with certain relatives. You may get closer to someone, for example, who is extremely helpful or who seems to have the same parenting style as you. This can be a good thing, but it can make other family members upset about the new family dynamics. Don't make excuses or try to hide what's going on. Provide a simple explanation, without getting defensive, then let everyone adjust on their own.

- Just because certain family members haven't visited each other's homes or interacted with each other in the past doesn't mean they can't now. If given the chance, they might be willing to be more flexible in order to spend more time with the baby.

> *My husband and I were ready to take a vacation by ourselves when Corbin was nine months old. We decided to make plans to go to a bed and breakfast near the city where both of my divorced parents live. I scheduled the trip when my mom, my step-father, my father and my step-mother were all available. I made it clear from the beginning that I wanted them all to be able to spend time with Corbin, but that I wasn't going to be there to handle taking him from one house to the other. They were going to have to figure out a way to do it among themselves. I also made it clear that if anyone couldn't manage to do that, the other side of the family would just keep him the whole time. After ten years of being totally unwilling to speak to each other, the four grandparents managed to work it all out amicably. They each had minor complaints about each other, but everyone survived the experience and was willing to do it again in the future.* (Brittany)

- If there are problems that involve your partners' family, get him to help solve them. If he's uncomfortable about getting involved, remind him that he has a responsibility to be supportive of his immediate family—you and your baby—not just his extended family. He'll probably have good insight into how to make things better. Your in-laws will probably also be more understanding if information comes from him.

- There is no way you can make everyone happy, let alone make everyone happy all at the same time. Let go of that dream right away. You'll get incredibly stressed if you try to achieve that unrealistic goal.

- The truth is always the best answer. Even if someone isn't happy with it, it's generally better to be honest that to try to make up a story to protect someone's feelings.

  My mother has never gotten along with my mother-in-law. Once when Rockey and I were going out of town for a weekend, we asked his mother to baby-sit Tory. I told my mother that we were taking the baby with us. Unfortunately, one of my mother-in-law's friends ran into my mother at a store and told her how much my mother-in-law had enjoyed spending the weekend with the baby. My mother was furious for weeks. Had I just told her in the first place, she might have been a little upset for a few days, but I wouldn't have had to spend months trying to regain her trust. (Anne)

- Remind family members of the saying, "If you can't say something nice, don't say anything at all." Never let people bad-mouth other family members in front of your child. This is good practice for when your baby is a toddler and repeats everything he hears, regardless of who is listening.

- If family members start arguing in front of your baby, you have choices about how to stop it. Tell them that you won't tolerate arguments in front of your baby, so they can either stop, they can leave or you and the baby can leave. Babies can sense stress. Whether she's bothered by loud voices or just feels your tension, it's not worth letting your baby get upset because other people can't get along.

- When family members criticize how much time other family members are spending with your baby, help them focus on the quality of time they spend with him, rather than the quantity. Ask what specific things they would like to do with the baby, invite them to share special times with you and provide opportunities for them to play with the baby, not just take care of him or be with him at events that don't allow for a lot of interaction.

Making Career-Oriented Transitions

Making career choices when you're a new mother is a complex challenge full of unanticipated emotions. Plans made during pregnancy may not feel exactly right once the baby is born. The most committed career woman may experience an unexpected desire to change her work so she can spend more time with her baby. A woman who was thrilled to stay home with her baby may eventually find that she misses working more than she imagined. Even women who had a relatively easy time deciding whether or not to return to work often find that implementing their decision is harder than they expected.

Since it's very difficult to know exactly what your career options are, let alone whether they'll meet your personal preferences, this chapter helps you explore a full-range of possibilities, from full-time work to flexible part-time work to no work at all. With the number and flexibility of options available in today's marketplace, the chances are good that you can find a way to achieve your own version of life and career balance if you choose to work. If you decide to be a professional mom—what some might call a stay-at-home mom—there are ways to ease the transition, love what you're doing and preserve your career options for the future.

Your decision-making shouldn't be about having to give up either career growth or time with your baby. It should be about identifying the most important aspects of work and motherhood, then creating a scenario that meets your unique needs and wants.

CHAPTER NINETEEN

Evaluating Your Career and Life Balance Choices

You have to consider your lifestyle and personal goals if you want to make a successful professional decision. If you aren't careful you're liable to find yourself with some significant regrets years from now. Trust me on this. As a career consultant, I coach lots of baby boomers with twenty years of experience in industries and jobs they now hate. They inevitably express the wish that they had made career choices that made them happy and gave them life balance back when they were younger. Many are now trying to make career transitions to create more time with their teen-aged kids. Since you're in the process of making a career choice anyway, you might as well make one that meets your personal preferences and professional goals.

Whether you're leaning toward taking any job that provides the desired income and schedule, trying to stay within your career path or considering taking a break from working, the suggestions in this chapter will help you handle the situation strategically. This will increase your chances of making the right decision. If you decide to work, it will also make it easier, faster and less stressful to get the type of employment situation you want. But even if you have to compromise in some ways, you'll feel more satisfied with your choice when you know that what you gave up is less important than what you got.

- You can't determine which career option is best until you know what you want. Since it's a good idea to consider the future when you're planning for today, think about what you want now and think you'll want in the future. Just recognize that your preferences and situation may change down the road, so the plans you make today should be flexible enough to adapt to the future reality. This suggestion applies whether you're making plans while you're pregnant or your baby has already been born.

- Following are the types of questions you should ask yourself—and answer truthfully—in order to figure out if and how you want to balance career and motherhood.

  ❏ How much income do you need or want to earn (short-term and long-term, definite and potential)?

  ❏ Are you going to feel guilty if you don't work? Will you feel guilty if you do?

  ❏ How do you feel about child care?

  ❏ Do you want to continue to do the same type of work you've been doing?

  ❏ Will you feel proud of what you're doing if you work outside your profession?

  ❏ How do you feel about taking a break from your career?

  ❏ Can you be satisfied and fulfilled if you don't work? How about if you do work?

  ❏ Do you plan on working in a full-time, traditional role when your children are in school?

  ❏ Do you want to work part-time so you can be home when your children come home from school?

- Use the answers to these questions to create a detailed profile of the ideal work scenario. Just dream, don't worry about reality, but include realistic criteria such as:

  WORKSTYLE: hours, location, schedule, legalities

  JOB DESCRIPTION: type, amount and level of responsibility, similarity or difference from your previous experience

CAREER PATH: industry, professional level, future opportunities

PERSONAL SATISFACTION: pride in the job, sense of accomplishment, enjoyment of the actual work, career goals

MOTHERHOOD STYLE: amount of time with your baby, child care preferences

FINANCIAL RESPONSIBILITIES: income, tax implications

Be sure to include what's right for the current situation and what you think may be right in the future. It's even a good idea to prioritize the criteria that are most important to you.

> *When I was pregnant and daydreaming about staying home with my baby, I felt guilty for thinking of jumping off the corporate ladder. How could I consider letting my expensive college education go to waste? I thought working was an all or nothing proposition. After my maternity leave was over and I was back at work full-time, I sat down and analyzed all my career and life priorities. I realized that guilt was getting in the way of getting what I really wanted. It's incredibly important that I'm able to be home with my child, now when she's a baby and later when she comes home from school. I decided that work schedule was a bigger priority than prestigious job titles. I found a part-time job in the same field, so I'm using my professional expertise, but I won't make partner. I can't believe how much better I feel about my new version of life/career balance.* (Marissa)

> *After my baby was born, I made a prioritized list of the top ten most important criteria in a job. Then, I defined the kind of role and the type of company that would be likely to meet those criteria. Instead of being a secretary for a law firm, I decided to work for the school district. That way, I'd have lots of vacation time, I'd be with lots of other moms and I would get good benefits. I still work full-time, but I'm much happier. I make less money, but I also have lower child-care expenses since my baby is with me more often.* (Rachel)

- Both you and your partner became parents. If you both want to achieve career and life balance, you must factor both of your needs and desires into the equation. The family's need for income must be defined. Each of your short and long-term career goals should be discussed. All the options, including either one or both of you changing your workstyle or position, should be identified and evaluated.

- Once you've defined what you want, you can evaluate the various career/life balance options according to how well they can provide it. You should consider all the options that are potentially available to you, not just the ones that seem the easiest and most logical right now. Your options include staying in the same job, changing the schedule or other parameters of your current job, finding the same type of job with another employer, making a career transition into a new type of position and/or industry, taking a job outside your area of expertise or career path in order to meet certain schedule or income needs, starting your own business, freelancing, consulting and not working at all.

- Employers' attitudes and modern technology have opened up an unprecedented realm of possibilities for how, when and where you work. The sheer number of options can make your decision more difficult, but if you decide to work, your chances of creating a lifestyle that suits your preferences are better than ever before.

- There's a lot of effort and information involved in defining what you want and evaluating how well various work options fulfill those goals. Write things down so you can track your progress and make informed decisions.

- You're making so many changes in your life right now. Let your natural personality style help you decide how much of a career change you feel comfortable making. If you like to make all your big changes at once, go for it! If that sounds a bit overwhelming for you, take smaller steps towards your goals.

- If you're considering taking a break now but continuing on your professional career path in the future, you need to determine now how a gap in your career history will affect you. Don't guess about what might happen if you slow your climb up the proverbial ladder. Get the facts. Talk to people who are in the type of role you eventually hope to have. Conduct informational interviews with human resource professionals in your field.

- Another method to determine how a change in your workstyle will affect your career growth is to talk with women in your field who seem to be doing a good job of achieving life and career balance. Ask them how they manage their careers and families. How did they adjust their workstyles to adapt to their family responsibilities? Attend meetings of your professional organizations, ask for referrals from human resource managers and network with your friends in order to find people to talk with. Most women will be flattered by your interest. If not, you probably don't want their advice anyway.

- If you have difficulty identifying and/or assessing your work or career options, it might be helpful to meet with a career coach. Look in the yellow pages under "career" and/or "consultants." Set free initial consultations with several different consultants. Make sure to select a coach who will help you define and evaluate your career choices, not just conduct a job search.

- The career choice you make now doesn't commit you forever. If what you chose doesn't work out for you, you can re-evaluate yourself and the market and make another choice. Just make sure to evaluate what went wrong last time so you don't make the same mistake again.

- The same goes if you decide to take a break from working. You can still change your mind at any time in the future. If you decide to go back to work, potential employers will understand the gap in your employment history. If they don't understand, they don't share your personal value system so you probably wouldn't like working there anyway.

- Even if you make the best possible choice for your situation now, when your child is a baby, you may find that your preferences and priorities change during future stages of motherhood. Different career options may become more or less appealing over time. Re-evaluate your career and life balance choices whenever you're feeling curious about other possibilities.

CHAPTER TWENTY

Getting What You Want From Working

New Workstyle Options

New ways of working are being developed all the time as technology and corporate expectations evolve. This is a great time to be creative and innovative in how, when and where you do your work. Just be sure to evaluate the pros and cons of the various workstyle options as realistically as possible. One really big positive may or may not outweigh all the smaller negatives. As you evaluate the choices, frequently refer back to your definition of the most important aspects of what you want and need.

- One of the best options is to create a job description that clearly defines what outcomes you'll generate and when they'll be completed, but leaves you with the flexibility about where and when you get the work done.

- Within a somewhat traditional work environment, you may be able to be creative with your schedule. Skip lunch so you can leave earlier in the afternoon or work longer shifts four days a week so you can take one day off, for example.

- Sometimes a change in your work status will help you obtain the work schedule you desire. As an independent contractor or a freelancer, for example, instead of an employee, you are in control of when you work. If you select this option, be sure to research how other people in your field structure and charge for their work. Hourly rates for an employee and an independent contractor are very different!

- Working part-time can be a great way to balance your personal and professional lives. Just make sure that you and your co-workers adjust your expectations about what you can now accomplish in your time at work. Also evaluate what you and your partner think you can do at home. Everyone involved can end up feeling stressed if too much is expected. Instead of being a method to give you the best of both worlds, you can end up with the worst.

- Working at home is another option that can create stress, rather than reduce it, if the situation isn't handled properly. Don't expect to be able to work and care for your baby at the same time. Neither activity will get the attention it deserves. Schedule work periods into your day when she's asleep or someone else is available to care for her. You'll still be there if she needs you for nursing or for comfort, you can use the time you would have spent commuting for quality time with your baby, and you'll have the benefit of working in a relaxed, comfortable environment.

- If you plan on working at home, remember that your baby will sleep less as he gets older. Nap times may not continue to provide enough work time. Start researching your child care options when he's very young so you'll be prepared when you need it.

- There are lots of legal and insurance issues related to telecommuting, working as a sub-contractor, job sharing, and other newer workstyles. Talk with the human resource department, your lawyer, your insurance agent and/or other people who work under similar conditions to make sure you've covered all the bases.

- If you want to work on an occasional, rather than a regular basis, and you have very flexible child care, you could sign up with a temporary agency. Ask human resource managers, people in your field of work and career consultants to recommend specialists in your industry or profession.

Adapting Your Current Job

Once you've defined your ideal workstyle, you can try to adapt your existing job to fit. In today's work environment, many employers are receptive to alternatives to full-time work at the work site. It's usually easier to change your current job than to go out and look for a new job. It's worth a try, anyway.

- If you think your boss won't be at all open to the idea of alternative work options, be careful when discussing it with her. You don't want her to think that you're unhappy with your job and likely to leave soon —unless you are unhappy and will leave, that is.

- Be clear, with your boss and yourself, about what you'll do if your existing job can't be changed to suit your new needs. Will you stay or not?

- When you talk with your boss about restructuring your job, focus on the needs of the company and the results you can create, not on your personal situation. No matter how good a friend she is and how much she wants to help you, the boss isn't responsible for addressing your motherhood-related issues. Be clear about what changes you'd like made, help her figure out ways to make it work for you and the company, and be open to her ideas about alternatives.

> *My boss and I agreed that I could continue to work on a part-time contract basis, but the hourly rate they were offering was lower than I wanted. My first instinct was to explain that I wouldn't keep working for them unless I made more than enough to cover my child care expenses. A career counselor helped me realize that I should use my credentials, experience with the company, and my willingness to work within their inconvenient schedule as negotiating points. Not only did they raise the rate, but they give me as much work as I want. (Joan)*

- Approach your boss with a list of options and suggestions, not demands. Try to have a conversation, not a negotiation. If you convey a win-win attitude it will help your boss be open-minded and flexible.

- If your boss is reluctant to make changes in your work schedule, research other companies in your industry. Define what has worked for them. Help your employer determine how to make the scenario work for both of you. Don't expect her to figure it out herself if there isn't a precedent.

Conducting a Job Search

It's never fun to look for a new job. It's even harder when you're a new mom. If you can't get what you want any other way, though, you'll just have to try to stay organized and focused in the midst of piles of laundry, a fussy baby, an unpredictable schedule and sheer exhaustion. Following are some tips to help you handle the aspects of a job search that are affected by your responsibilities as a mother.

- Think about your skills and experience. The strengths you want to use may be different that the ones you could use. For example, you may decide you want a relaxing job that doesn't require a lot of brain power. As you seek jobs and communicate with potential employers, only provide information on skills that fit with the type of work you want to do.

- If you're looking specifically for companies that offer family-friendly benefits and attitudes, look for lists in local business newspapers and magazines, chamber of commerce publications and national magazines that target new moms and working women. Another way to identify good companies is to network with working women who have young children.

- Set aside certain times in your day or week to work on your job search. You'll never get to it if you just try to fit it in whenever you can.

- Make your child care arrangements before you actually find a job so you'll know what work schedule you can accept when you talk to potential employers.

- If you have to leave messages for people to call you back, leave specific ranges of time when they should call. If your baby is consistent about when he naps, you can use those times. Otherwise, get a baby-sitter or try to get him calmly playing by himself in a safe place during those times. This allows you to be prepared to take important calls without interruptions.

- When you negotiate with a potential employer, keep your personal needs, such as your child care provider's schedule, to yourself. If you have a specific time frame in which you can work, that's all you need to say. Don't get into the details of your home situation. Not only does she really not care at this point, but it may bring up concerns about how you will balance your professional and personal responsibilities.

- If a potential employer asks about how you will balance motherhood and working, be as positive and reassuring as possible, even though she probably shouldn't be asking this type of question. Tell her that you have your support system set up so you can be totally focused on the job when you're working. That's all she really needs to know, not the details of how you're going to manage it.

- Stay focused on getting what's really important to you. If you don't, you'll probably end up referring back to this section again before long.

I kept a written, prioritized list of the most important criteria for a new job posted on my bathroom mirror. It motivated me in the morning to keep trying for what I really wanted. It helped me evaluate my progress at the end of the day. It encouraged me to turn down a job offer that just wasn't a good match. I ended up getting a job that had the responsibilities, income and most importantly, the schedule I wanted so I could be with Lexi as much as possible. (Kay)

CHAPTER TWENTY-ONE

Returning to Work

The feelings that new mothers have when they return to work run the gamut from "Thank God, I couldn't take another day at home," to "I'm doing irreparable damage to my child by not staying at home," to "I'm glad to be back at work, but I miss my baby." All these feeling are normal. So much has changed in your life that it would be unnatural for you not to have strong feelings about returning to work. It's a very stressful time, but knowing what to expect makes the emotions easier to deal with. Planning ahead makes the transition smoother.

- Scrap your old schedule. Have your partner scrap his, too. Start over from scratch. Consider factors such as the time necessary for you, your partner and the baby to get dressed and fed, the child care provider's schedule, commutes to and from child care and work, and your new energy level.

  Jake and I used to get together with friends on weeknights, after we both got home from work. Now that we have Elliot, we want to be with him in the evenings. Some of our friends who have lighter schedules seemed to have a little trouble getting used to our new routine, but it works for us. We just want to relax at home and play with our baby. (Joyce)

  Henry and I work full-time. We leave at 7:00 am and often don't get back until after 6:00 pm. We let Christopher stay up until 9:00 so we have time to play with him. He takes longer naps than many eight

143

month-olds, so we know he's getting enough sleep, but people keep telling us that we'll have trouble getting him to bed early when he's older. We've decided that we'll deal with that problem if and when it arises. For now, this schedule works for us. (Tricia)

- Share your excitement and your pictures with your co-workers for the first few days, then put your pictures on your desk or in your wallet and get back to work. The longer you spend being the new mother at work, the harder it might be to break that stereotype when you're ready to get serious.

- If you're pumping breastmilk, be considerate of work schedules. Use your breaks and lunch hours if you're required to report time on an hourly basis. Your employer does not owe you special breaks in addition to the regular ones. You also don't want co-workers to resent your absences.

- Finding trustworthy, convenient daycare can be a long, traumatic experience. The suggestions in Section Twelve will help make the process easier, but I strongly encourage you to start looking months before you'll actually need it. It's also a good idea to try it out before you actually need to go back to work to make sure everything is working out for you and your baby.

   I knew that dropping Robbie off at child care the first time was going to be very emotional for me. Since I didn't want to show up at work with red eyes and mascara running down my cheeks, I did a couple of test runs before I started back to work. I only left him for a couple of hours the first few times. I think this strategy helped both of us adjust. (Jan)

- Make arrangements for when your baby is sick before she's sick. Arrange with a friend, family member, baby-sitting service or other child care provider to be on call for those times when your baby has something minor enough that you don't feel that you need to stay home with her, but significant enough that she can't go to her usual child care provider. You can also use this back-up system if your child care provider gets sick or can't take care of your baby for some other reason.

- If your baby will be switching from nursing to a bottle, introduce the bottle at least a couple of weeks before you return to work. This ensures that both you and your baby have the opportunity to make the transition with as little stress as possible.

- Resist any temptations to make sudden career changes when you first return to work. Give yourself some time to get used to the new routines. If you've been back at work for at least a month and you're still having a really hard time with either the logistics or the emotions that are involved, re-evaluate your career/life balance choices. Then you can make strategic rather than impulsive changes.

- If you find yourself feeling guilty that you are doing neither your job nor your duties as a mother as well as you'd like, focus on what you can improve, not just on what's wrong. Identify what you can and can't control, review your options, remind yourself about what's most important to you and commit yourself to making choices that help you balance your personal and professional life in a satisfying manner. It may not be easy, but the results will be worth it.

- If your current work is different than your long-term career goal, try to stay in contact with the future market. Network with professional associations, stay in contact with friends in the field and read trade publications, for example. This will make it much easier to understand the target market when you're ready to return to it.

What to Try: To Make Going Back to Work Easier

ACKNOWLEDGE YOUR FEELINGS about returning to work, your new role as a working mother and your concerns about child care to yourself and to others.

TALK TO OTHER WORKING NEW MOTHERS about their feelings, experiences and tips for adjusting.

EASE YOURSELF BACK INTO WORK, if possible. Start with fewer hours and work your way up to the full schedule.

MAKE YOUR FIRST DAY BACK AT WORK A WEDNESDAY, Thursday or Friday. That way, your first week back at work won't seem too long for you or your baby.

REVIEW YOUR ROUTINE. Are you trying to do too much? Is it getting in the way of spending quality time with your baby and your partner, as well as by yourself?

EXAMINE YOUR LIFE for activities, efforts and commitments that could be eliminated in order to make more time. Learn to say "no." Carefully weigh your choices regarding extra-curricular activities. Delay some activities until your baby is older.

PUT YOUR BABY IN A CHILD CARE SETTING THAT'S CLOSE to work so you can spend more time together in the car before and after work.

OR PUT YOUR BABY IN A CHILD CARE SETTING THAT'S CONVENIENT for both you and your partner. You've made a lots of adjustments in your life lately. Your partner can and should adapt his before and after work routines to include some baby-care responsibilities.

SET LIMITS AT WORK. Set new work hours, limit travel, define how early and late you'll work or do some of your work at home when the baby is asleep. Be sure that in addition to setting these new limits, you communicate them to your co-workers.

IF YOU FIND YOURSELF MISSING YOUR BABY A LOT, STAY IN TOUCH with him. Put pictures on your desk, in your purse and on your key chain. Phone the baby-sitter and, if possible, talk to your baby once or twice during the day. Visit him during the lunch hour. This is an especially good idea if you want to continue nursing as much as possible.

IF THINKING ABOUT THE BABY IS DISTRACTING YOU FROM YOUR WORK, PUT PICTURES OF HER OUT OF SIGHT. Out of sight doesn't necessarily mean out of mind, of course, but this might help reduce the number of times your concentration is broken. Focus on work at work and on the baby when you're with her.

MAKE A VIDEO OR AUDIO TAPE OF YOURSELF reading a book, singing or talking to your baby so he can see or hear you while you're gone.

HELP YOUR OLDER BABY SETTLE INTO A SCHEDULE THAT ENABLES YOU TO SEE HER. For example, if you get home at six-thirty, a seven o'clock bedtime won't leave you much time together. It's more important for you to have time with your baby than for her to be on a traditional schedule. Just be careful that she gets enough sleep during the day and that she doesn't stay up so late that you and your partner don't get any time alone.

REMIND YOURSELF that the income you earn by working is helping to support your child and that children of working mothers can grow up just fine.

MAKE EVERY MOMENT WITH YOUR BABY COUNT. Time spent in the car before and after work is a great time to talk, sing, point out objects and interact with your baby. Diaper time can be a time for a special song or playing *This Little Piggy*. Play your own silly little game for helping your baby learn the names of his body parts while you get him dressed. Have fun whenever you can.

CHAPTER TWENTY-TWO

Becoming a Professional Mom

Becoming a professional mom can be a surprisingly emotional transition, even if it's exactly what you wanted. The adjustment can affect how you think of yourself and everything you do. It can be especially difficult if you always pictured yourself as a working woman and built your personal identity around what you do professionally.

The major difference you're likely to encounter is that being at home with a baby is totally different than being home alone used to be. At first it's like a vacation. Even though you're incredibly busy with baby-related activities, the freedom to totally focus on the baby and forget about schedules, work responsibilities and other activities is wonderful. I urge you to be careful, though. Even if you don't mean to, it's easy to lose touch with all your other interests, activities and friends while you're enjoying being with your baby.

If you let your whole life revolve only around your baby for too long, you might start to feel like something is missing—you! You may suddenly realize that the person pushing the baby stroller through the mall in the middle of the day doesn't feel like the same person who used to generate tangible results, be involved in important meetings, talk to other adults about substantive topics and contribute to the family's finances.

My suggestion for avoiding this emotional pitfall is to regularly remind yourself that deciding to be a professional mom doesn't mean that's all you can be. Not everything has to be for and with the baby. Make a conscious effort to re-arrange your life in a way that supports your on-going interests while you enjoy your role as a mom. Nurture yourself as an individual. Not only will you enjoy your role as a mother while your child is a baby, but you'll also find it easier to be productive and fulfilled, whether or not that means returning to work, when your child goes off to school.

- Give yourself a maternity leave, with a defined time limit, just like you would if you were returning to work. During this time, it's totally natural to focus primarily on the baby. After all, you have a lot of recuperating, adjusting and learning to do. Once that time period is over, it helps to think of yourself as having a new job—motherhood. Just like any other job, you can't be 100% focused on it 100% of the time. You need breaks and other activities or you're likely to get burned out.

- There's nothing wrong with making some baby-sitting or child care arrangements on a regular basis. You deserve some free time that you probably won't get otherwise.

  After seven months at home with Cody, I was desperate for some time alone in the house. My husband would stay home so I could go out occasionally, but he couldn't understand why sometimes I wanted him to take Cody out with him for a while. I had to explain that it isn't relaxing while the baby is napping. I'm constantly listening for him, expecting him to wake up, hoping he'll sleep a little longer. I wanted some time when I was absolutely sure I wouldn't be interrupted while I was doing whatever I chose to do. (Reesa)

- Not only should you continue with activities that have always been important to you, but you should also seek out activities that address the needs and interests that used to be fulfilled through working.

- Remember to consider options that didn't work for you when you were working. A new hobby or interest may be realistic now that your schedule is more flexible.

- Exercise, join special interest clubs, volunteer, take classes and stay in touch with friends who aren't moms in order to satisfy yourself as a woman, not just a mother.

> *My mother was a full-time, stay-at-home mother her whole life. The only activities she got involved in had to do with her kids' school or sports programs. She has a hard time understanding that I don't feel completely satisfied unless I'm involved with activities that don't revolve around my baby. I think it's because she always planned to be a wife and mother. I grew up with specific, work-oriented goals. Now that I have a baby, I realize that working while my kids are young isn't the lifestyle I want. Even though I'm not working, I don't want my entire identity to revolve around my role as a mother. I still think of myself as a professional woman.* (Gwen)

- A great way to meet other new mothers and their babies is to enroll in a post-partum exercise class or a mother-tot play class. Community centers, recreation centers, athletic clubs and religious organizations often sponsor these types of programs.

- If you know other new mothers, form a playgroup to get some adult conversation. Even though your baby is far too young to socialize, you'll enjoy the interaction and, perhaps, form lasting friendships.

> *Another new mother that I had met a few times at synagogue invited me to join a playgroup she was forming. Those weekly get-togethers became so important that I began planning everything else around playgroup times. Both Tara and I have made friends for life.* (Marcie)

- Remember to stay in touch with friends who aren't moms. Try to discuss topics that don't relate to your baby. This will help you get some of the adult conversations you're probably craving.

> *I'm hooked on e-mail. I also go into a few chat rooms to "talk." The computer gives me a way to interact with other people whenever I have the time.* (Chanelle)

- If you were used to working full-time, it may seem strange to be having fun and running errands during the day. Your routines are set up for the time before and after work. You may feel like an impostor when you go to the store during the day. Is that really you in the mall instead of at work at two-thirty in the afternoon? It will probably take a conscious effort on your part to re-define how you use your time. If it isn't enough just to remind yourself that you don't have to wait for evenings and weekends to get things done, make a list of all the activities you want and need to do. Then schedule them out on a calendar, making sure that you've spread them out evenly across the days and evenings. You'll probably only need to do this once or twice before you get the hang of it.

- A common frustration for stay-at-home moms is that they don't have many opportunities to feel a sense of completion. As soon as all the laundry is done, something else is dirty. The minute you finish cleaning the house, something spills. Everything is on-going, repetitive activity. If this bothers you, one solution is to find a volunteer project or personal activity that involves concrete goals, a beginning, middle and end, and outcomes. Another suggestion is to create goals and plans for the repetitive aspects of motherhood. For example, you can try to finish the laundry by 3:00 so you have time to meet a friend for coffee. Or you can set a schedule so that certain chores, such as laundry or heavy-duty housecleaning are done at specific times on a regular basis. Then, when something is done, you won't have to do it again for a while.

- Even if you've been following my advice and staying active with non-mommy activities and interests, it's frustrating to realize that other people only see you as a mom. (Was the trail of spit-up running down the back of your sweatshirt their first clue??) You may want to yell out that there's more to you than being a mom! Sure you love motherhood, but you also want to be seen as an intelligent, productive, involved woman. I promise, the two aren't mutually exclusive. Remind yourself that it's okay for others to see you as just a mom because you know there's more to you than that. If that doesn't help, increase how involved you are in non-mommy activities. Maybe then you'll feel so fulfilled as a person that you won't care what other people think of you.

   I have a hard time answering the question, "What do you do?" I feel strange saying that I'm a lawyer, since I'm not being one right now. But saying "I'm a mom" doesn't feel right, either. It also seems to direct the conversation toward my kids instead of towards me. I would die before saying that I'm a housewife. My best solution so far is to say that I'm a lawyer, but that I'm taking a break to raise my kids. (Stacey)

- If you're bothered that motherhood seems to be all that you are right now, remind yourself that being a great mom involves a lot of intelligence and that you make a major contribution to our society when you raise a smart, well-rounded, moral and productive child. Also remember that you haven't lost any aspects of who you used to be, you've just added motherhood to your list of skills. While motherhood may be overwhelming your sense of yourself right now, that's not all you are.

- Adjusting to having less income can be a tricky transition. I encourage you and your partner to discuss financial matters before a problem arises. Consider your overall family expenses, including existing and upcoming baby-related costs, your own personal needs and the way cash flow is handled. Agree on the way you will each make financial decisions, manage the money and pay regular and unexpected expenses.

     Bob and I used to have separate and joint bank accounts and expenses. When I first stopped working after Dylan was born, we tried making little adjustments in how we handled the money. Bob started putting a little more in the joint checking account. Then he gave me some money to help me pay my credit card bills. He started feeling out of control since he never knew how much money I would need. I felt guilty about spending his money on myself. Things got much better when we decided to make all the money and the expenses ours instead of his or mine. (Pam)

- Don't be surprised to find that you're occasionally bored. There are two kinds of boredom. One kind happens when you're doing the same baby care responsibilities over and over again. The other kind happens when you've finished all the books you stocked up on, the baby is napping and you're home doing the laundry, instead of out having fun. It happens. Once you get a little more used to life with a baby, you'll be able to develop more things you can do at home or with the baby. It just takes a little time and effort. Talk to other mothers. Either they'll have ideas about what to do or you can be bored over the phone together.

     My girlfriend and I missed getting together after our babies were born. We could never coordinate times to go out and have fun. Rather than totally give up seeing each other, we decided to start running our errands together. Going grocery shopping wasn't as much fun as going to the movies, but we were still accomplishing something and being with each other. Our husbands thought we were pathetic, but it worked for us. (Nicole)

- A day at home with a baby is very different than a day at home without one. Make sure you and your partner have realistic expectations about what you can accomplish. Going to the grocery store, the post office and running a few errands can be major accomplishments on some days. Don't feel silly for being proud of achieving your new goals. If your partner doesn't understand, encourage him to try to get things done while he spends a whole day caring for the baby. Of course, I think he should do this even if he is understanding and supportive. It's good for all of you!

- When you're home, it's easy to snack all day long. That's fine as long as you snack on healthy treats. Eating too much junk food, however, might make it difficult for you to satisfy your nutritional requirements, not to mention lose any weight. If you have trouble keeping track of how many snacks you eat, put out an appropriate amount of snacks at the beginning of each day. When those snacks are gone, you've snacked enough. It also helps to reduce the amount of junk food in your home.

- Foster your feelings of professionalism in order to maintain your sense of individuality and adulthood. Continue to use your daytimer, remain aware of trends in your field by reading trade journals and attending association meetings, and/or apply your skills as a volunteer with a non-profit organization.

- You may find that some of your professional friends or family members, especially those who returned to work after the birth of their babies, treat you differently now. They might not understand your choice. They may actually be jealous that you were able to do what they really wanted to do, even if they can't admit it. You may end up feeling somewhat guilty and doubt the choice you made after you talk with them. Remind yourself, and them, about why you decided to stay home. It might also be helpful to see those friends when your baby is with a baby-sitter. If someone still can't seem to respect your new lifestyle, she may not be that good a friend after all.

My mom is a hard-core, baby boomer "Supermom." She became a high-powered vice president of a Fortune 500 corporation while raising three kids. She's being supportive, but deep down I know she thinks I should have waited until I had moved up the corporate ladder before having a baby. What really makes her crazy is that I'm going to stay home with Kelly and any future babies for a few years. I can't imagine being as busy and stressed as she was. I also know what it's like to be in daycare all day. That's not what I want for my family. My career will have to wait. (Sara)

- If you might eventually want to go back to work for your previous employer, tell them. Let them know that you will contact them when the time is right. Stay in touch through holiday cards, continued friendships with former co-workers and occasional calls to touch base with your former boss. Make sure to stay in contact with more than one person in the company, just in case your primary contact leaves.

- If you were on a paid maternity leave when you decided not to return to work, carefully evaluate your choices about how you tell your employer. It doesn't have to be an all or nothing situation. If you think you might want to take off only a year or so, you could ask for an unpaid leave of absence. This keeps your options open for a while. If you take the benefits of a maternity leave, then quit, you'd better not have any intentions of returning to work there in the future.

- The gap in your employment history doesn't have to be a problem. In the future, when you communicate with potential employers, say something to the effect of, "When I had a baby, I decided to totally focus on my role as a mother. Now that I'm ready to return to work, I'm prepared to focus on my professional responsibilities." This type of statement conveys that you're in control of your choices and that you'll be just as committed to performing on the job as you were to raising your children.

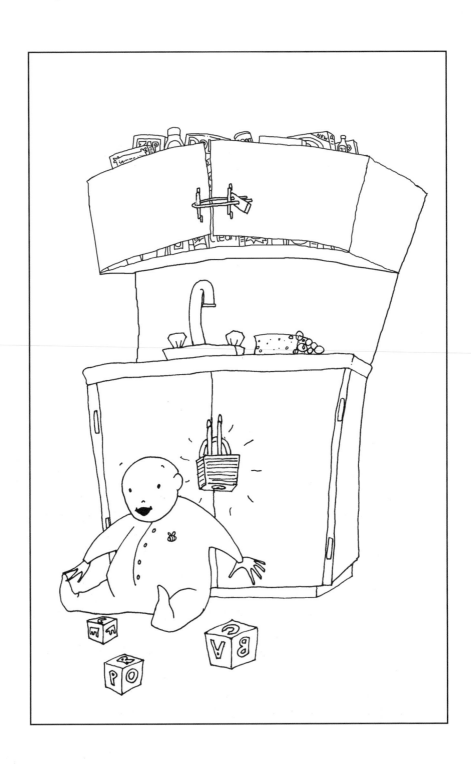

Creating a Safe Home Environment

Your responsibility for creating a safe home starts as soon as your baby comes home from the hospital. Although some aspects of baby proofing can wait until she can move around and get into things, there are many steps you need to take immediately and consistently to protect her. Remember that more accidents happen in the home than anywhere else. If you can imagine it, it can happen. If you think "maybe I should...," DO IT. If you think "what if...," takes steps to prevent it. Any inconveniences will only last for short time in the overall scheme of things.

The good news is that if you do it right, organizing your home so it's safe for your baby has positive benefits for you, too. You'll be able to relax while she explores in safety. You won't have to remain vigilant at every moment. You'll also be able to leave her alone for a little while in certain areas. Oh, and you won't have to shout "no, don't touch" all the time. This freedom from constant, hovering attention is good for both of you!

CHAPTER TWENTY-THREE

The Baby's Things

The Baby's Room

The whole experience of becoming a mother seems so real as you organize all the paraphernalia and set up the room. The smell of fresh paint and the sight of tiny, carefully-folded T-shirts lying in a drawer have the power to bring tears to a new mother's eyes. There's nothing like the first time you take the baby into his new room and place him in his crib. The excitement of the newly redecorated room can wear off quickly, though, if the furniture, supplies and decorations aren't arranged in a way that's safe for your baby and convenient for you.

One day, exactly three weeks before my due date, I demanded that my husband move his desk and the guest bed out of the room that was to be the baby's. For weeks I had been asking him nicely to do it. I had finally had it. I wanted the stuff moved immediately. Not half an hour after he had finished, my water broke. Six hours later, Jordan was born. A few hours after that, Andy called the baby store to tell them to deliver the furniture that I had previously ordered. He and my mother set up the whole room while I was in the hospital. When I came home, the first thing I did was take the baby up to his room. Seeing him lying in the crib, with the toys and sheets I had so carefully chosen, made the reality of the new situation sink in. I cried with joy. (Sheryl)

- It's okay to arrange your newborn's room based only on how it looks as long as you're willing to arrange it for more practical reasons once she's mobile. If you prefer to arrange the room more permanently, plan around what your baby will be able to do and reach when she's a toddler. During the first year or so, you can make changes as needed. After that, many babies prefer that their environment remains the same.

- The baby's room doesn't have to be right next to yours. If you're concerned about being able to hear him cry, use baby monitors.

- Arrange the room so you have easy access to the crib and the changing table. You don't want to step over toys or bump into a table when you go in during the middle of the night.

- Consider whether you're right-handed or left-handed. For example, if you're going to use your left hand to hold the baby's feet while you change the diaper, you want the things you need to be to your right, so you can grab them with your right hand.

> *My mother was a great help when I was getting the nursery ready for Jesse. In addition to helping me arrange the furniture, she offered to put all the diapers, wipes, receiving blankets and stuff I needed for routine baby care into the changing table. She arranged everything according to what I would need to use most frequently. The only problem was that she's right-handed and I'm a lefty. I had to reverse everything to make it convenient for me. (Sammy)*

- If possible, position the changing table close to the closet. That way, you can grab the clothes off the rack just before you put the baby down on the changing table. It's also handy if you store your extra diapers and wipes in the closet.

- Once your baby is mobile, keep the diaper pail in a place where she can't get into it or knock it over. You can keep it in the closet or, if you don't like the diaper smells in with the clean clothes, just put it on the changing table or dresser whenever your baby is playing in her room.

- The baby's room doesn't have to include a changing table, of course. You might find that it's easier to change the baby on the bathroom counter and keep the diaper pail in the bathroom.

> *I got sick of moving the diaper pail every time I left Iain in his room to play. I finally just moved it into the bathroom. Before long, I discovered*

that it was easier just to change him in there, too. Soon after that, I decided to keep some diapering supplies downstairs in a cabinet so I didn't always have to run upstairs to change him. I just threw away used diapers in the trash can in the garage. I felt stupid for doing things the "right" way for so long even though it was inconvenient in a lot of ways. (Addie)

- Never put the crib, the changing table or anything on which an adventuresome baby could climb next to a window.

- Stackable shelves, carts and other baby-proof items can be put on the floor in the closet. Since baby clothes are short, like the baby, you have plenty of usable space underneath them. It's also nice to store things in the closet because closing the door is an easy way to keep the baby away from things you don't want him to touch.

- Make sure that items in lower drawers are safe and that none of the furniture, lamps or decorations can be knocked over, pulled down or climbed upon.

- When you decorate the room, remember that your baby will keep getting taller and more mobile. Carefully select where you hang pictures and wall hangings. If you hang decorations over the crib or changing table, you'll probably have to move them later.

It was important to me to set up Leah's room so it was convenient for me and fun for her. I put up a wall-mounted Plexiglas mirror that ran the full length of the changing table. She loved looking at herself. I loved that she was happy and cooperative when I was diapering or dressing her. (Linda)

Toys

It's a shame that something intended to create pleasure could actually cause harm, but it's a reality. Even if a toy meets federal guidelines, it might not be safe for a baby under one year old. It's extremely important that you inspect new toys before you give them to your baby to make sure that they are safe and appropriate for her stage of development.

That alone, however, isn't good enough. You should also regularly check her toys and toys that she plays with at other people's houses to ensure that nothing is broken, dirty or inappropriate. The following suggestions will help you decide what your baby should and shouldn't be playing with.

- Be very careful about the toys you put in the crib. Crib toys, including stuffed animals, should be firm enough that your baby won't be smothered if his face ends up on them.

- Don't give your baby old-fashioned Fisher-Price Little People® (the small figures with a head and body—but no arms or legs—that fit into round holes in cars, trucks, farm sets and many other toys). The diameter of the old style Little People® toys is the same from top to bottom. This makes them a choking hazard. New Little People® have larger heads and wider bodies to prevent them from lodging in a baby's throat.

- Before you give a stuffed animal to your baby, test the eyes, nose, buttons, ribbons, bows and other attachments to make sure that they won't come off. When in doubt, either save the toy until your baby is old enough not to put small items in her mouth or remove the unsafe features.

- Beware of hand-crafted toys. While they may be darling, artists might not be aware of safety guidelines. Cords may be too long (over seven inches), paint unsafe, parts too small, etc.

- Age labeling on toys tends to relate to safety, not to how developmentally appropriate the toy is. Toy labels that indicate the toy is for children over three years of age might contain parts that are too small for your baby's safety. So, avoid these toys even if you think your baby would have fun playing with them.

> *Right after Allison, my second child, was born, I showed Austin, my three year-old, how big something had to be for it to be safe for the baby. Together, we went through all his toys to put anything that wasn't safe for the baby away in his room. I told him that the rules were: (1) anything that was in the family room had to be safe for Allison to play with, (2) all toys in the family room were to be shared, and (3) anything that he didn't want to share with the baby had to be in his room. We*

started enforcing these rules as soon as the baby was born so that by the time Allison was actually old enough to pick up the toys and put them in her mouth, Austin had plenty of practice keeping the small or special toys where they belonged. (Danielle)

- As soon as your baby can pull to a stand, check the toys in the crib to ensure that there isn't anything that he could inadvertently or purposefully use to climb or fall out of bed.

- Balloons aren't toys. Uninflated balloons and rubber pieces from popped balloons are a serious choking hazard. The strings from helium balloons aren't safe, either. Never leave your baby alone with a balloon.

  We turned letting go of a helium balloon outside into a game instead of a tragedy. We make a big deal about waving good-bye and watching it float away. That way Skyler never gets upset about losing a balloon and we never have to worry about having balloons in the house. (Carol)

- Choose a toy chest that either has a removable lid or a spring-loaded support that allows the top to remain open instead of falling shut.

- When you're given toys as gifts, there's nothing wrong with putting them away until your baby is old enough to appreciate them—even if the gift giver is right there. Don't take the risk of giving your baby an unsafe toy just to make someone else happy.

- An easy way to make sure that you'll use toys at the right time is to have boxes for different stages. As your baby develops new skills, pull out the toys in the appropriate box. This is also a great way to organize toys that have been handed down by friends and family members.

CHAPTER TWENTY-FOUR

General Home Safety

There are many precautions you can take at home to protect your baby's safety. There are so many, in fact, that you should consider the following section a sample of all the possibilities. There will probably be other potential hazards that are unique to your home and lifestyle.

- Post emergency phone numbers (doctor, poison control center, ambulance, etc.) on or near at least one phone in your house. It's also a good idea to have your address posted in an obvious location near the phone in case a baby-sitter or guest needs to direct emergency help to your home.

- If you don't have smoke detectors, install some. The batteries in your smoke detectors should be replaced twice a year. An easy way to remember to change them is to get into the habit of doing it when the clocks are adjusted each Spring and Fall.

- Minimize the amount of tobacco smoke to which your baby is exposed, at home and when you're out. Not only is smoke a contributing factor in respiratory illness, but recent studies indicate that exposure to smoke may also be a factor in SIDS (Sudden Infant Death Syndrome).

- Ingestion of lead can cause brain damage and other physical problems. Old paint on walls and furniture, painted clay or ceramic dishes (especially if they were made in another country), and water that runs through lead pipes are the usual sources. Test kits for paint and dishes

163

are available at hardware stores and some grocery stores. Your local water department or department of health can assist you to get your water tested.

- If you live in a home that was built before 1960, there are important steps you should take to prevent lead poisoning. Keep your baby out of the house during renovations, keep him away from areas where paint is chipped and frequently remove pieces of loose paint by washing window sills and other areas where the paint is cracking.

- Be extremely cautious about leaving your pet unsupervised around your baby. Even if your pet hasn't hurt a child before, it might react if it's feeling jealous or if its fur is being pulled. Continue to give your pet plenty of attention, supervise interaction between your pet and your baby and take your pet to obedience classes to minimize any potential problems.

- If you use disposable bottle inserts with tabs, remove the tabs before giving the bottle to baby. Your baby might not notice them for a long time, but the first time she does, she could pull them off and put them in her mouth. Even very young infants have the strength to pull off most tabs.

- Never put your baby to sleep with a pacifier leash attached to his clothing.

- Never tie a pacifier, toy or anything else on a cord around your baby's neck or waist.

- If your baby is very active in bed, use heavier pajamas instead of putting a blanket over her. The blanket could end up wrapped around her head.

- Fire retardant pajamas aren't made any longer, so don't be upset if you can't find them. Of the remaining options, synthetic sleepwear, while not as soft as cotton, is the least flammable.

- Don't use a sponge to wash your baby. He could easily bite off a piece and choke on it. Washcloths are safer.

- Be careful about wearing outfits with beads or other decorations on the shoulders or chest. Not only could they be uncomfortable for your baby's face, but she might be able to pull something off and swallow it.

- There are safety belts and harness straps on baby seats, swings, strollers and high chairs for a reason: they help keep your baby safe. Use them every time. Any momentary inconvenience you experience is nothing in comparison to the problems your baby might have if he falls.

- Never put your baby in a bouncer seat on a table or counter. She could use her feet to push herself backwards, bounce her way over to the edge or be knocked over the edge by something or someone. Don't risk it.

- Stop putting your baby in a bassinet or cradle once he can roll over or get up on his hands and knees. This type of equipment generally isn't stable enough to handle your baby's movements.

- I don't think baby jumpers that hang in a door frame are the best choice for entertaining your baby. If you want to use one anyway, wait until your baby can hold her head up well. Also make sure the molding is sturdy and the doorway is wide enough that she can't bang against the sides.

- Stop using a baby swing when your baby can lean forward and grab one of the legs of the stand or when he's heavier than the weight limit.

  Kyle loved his swing so much that I hated to stop using it, even though he was over the size limit. I finally realized that I had to put it away when he could lean over so far that he fell out. (Denise)

  Connor loved swinging so much that when he outgrew his baby swing, we bought an outdoor baby swing that we hung from the roof over the patio. (Crystal)

- Never leave the side of a mesh playpen folded down when your baby is in it. Not only could she roll or crawl out, but she could also get stuck and suffocate in between the folded-down side and the floor of the playpen. Regularly check the playpen's mesh and padding for holes that could entrap a baby's finger, toes or other body parts.

- As soon as your baby starts to push up onto his hands and knees, lower the mattress of the crib and remove any mobiles or baby toys that hang over the crib.

- Coins can easily choke a baby. Be extremely careful that loose change doesn't drop from pockets or purses. Regularly check underneath sofa cushions for fallen coins.

- Remember to put your closed purse away in a high place. Remind visitors to put their purses and belongings out of reach, too.

- Remind visitors not to put anything small, breakable or dangerous where the baby could get to it. Tell them exactly where the baby can reach. Also remind them to close doors, cabinets and safety gates securely if the baby is mobile.

- Never underestimate what your baby can do. Just because he couldn't do something yesterday doesn't mean that he won't be able to do it today. Just because the baby books say he won't be doing something for a few more weeks or months doesn't mean that your baby won't be able to do it much earlier. Be prepared far in advance.

- Walkers aren't very safe—even if you don't have any steps in your house. Even new walkers with a variety of updated safety features still let the baby to get into places that aren't safe and reach things that could be dangerous. Using a walker doesn't help your baby learn how to walk. The new alternatives which allow babies to swivel and bounce on a stationary base are safer and just as much fun.

- Teach "turn around and go feet first" from the beginning, as soon as your baby is mobile enough to try to go down a step or get off a bed or couch. Babies can't count or judge distance. If your baby learns that he can crawl forwards down a small step, it will be harder to teach him that he can't crawl off the bed or down a flight of stairs.

- When your baby is starting to try to pull up to a stand, move the crib mattress to its lowest level and remove the bumper pads.

- Don't be tempted to give your baby a pillow because you think it might be more comfortable for her. It's not safe for her to have one in her crib until she's one year old.

CHAPTER TWENTY-FIVE

Baby-Proofing

Baby proofing is a must. There's just no way that you can constantly have your eyes on your baby to ensure his safety each moment of every day. The awesome responsibility of this task will hit you as soon as your baby starts to move around. So will the realization that it's extremely difficult to anticipate every household safety risk when you're not sure exactly what a newly-mobile baby can and can't do.

Luckily, baby-proofing can be done in stages, instead of all at once. Your best bet is to get in the habit of surveying your home and making adjustments on a regular basis, preferably before your baby progresses to each new level of physical ability. It's a hassle to eliminate all the potential risks, but it's better than worrying about what could happen if you don't.

- It's okay to feel sad about putting a favorite memento out of sight. It's perfectly normal to be frustrated by the inconvenience of keeping frequently used products in hard-to-reach places. Nevertheless, baby-proofing is one area of parenthood in which your feelings don't matter much. It might make you less upset, though, to remember that these feelings are much easier to deal with than the horror of having your baby get hurt in an accident you could have prevented.

- Some new parents don't want to change everything in their home just because they have a baby. They're happy to take safety precautions, but don't want to move all their home decorations. It's fine to make this choice, just be aware that it will require you to be extra aware and vigilant. If you have plenty of time and the patience of a saint, you can start teaching your older baby not to touch certain objects, but it will probably be a lot less stressful to put special objects in a safe place until he's older. A baby less than one year old is too young to control her impulse to touch.

- If you're willing to baby-proof some, but not all of your house, make some rooms for adults only. Until your child is old enough to follow directions, block those unsafe rooms off with gates or doors.

- There are books on baby-proofing and services that will consult with you regarding your particular safety issues. If you're not sure about something, get help. You can find baby-proofing services by looking in the yellow pages under the "Baby Product—Retail" category.

  I hired a baby proofing company to come to my house to help me figure out what type of baby gate to put in an awkward place. I couldn't believe how many other safety hazards they found that I would never have thought of. It was worth every penny to have them come. (Kimberly)

- Items for baby-proofing your house can be obtained at toy stores, baby stores, safety supply companies, hardware stores, pet stores (where you can often find baby gates less expensively), child proofing companies or through baby goods catalogs or safety supply catalogs. Some resources are provided in the Resource Guide.

- Get on your hands and knees and crawl around your house. You'll probably notice hazards when you're on baby's level that you wouldn't have noticed from an adult's normal perspective.

  Baby-proofing and safety became major topics of discussion at playgroup once our babies were old enough to be crawling around and pulling up on the furniture. We were all hyper-aware of stories of babies being crushed by falling TV's, slipping off countertops and eating dangerous objects. We were obsessed with comparing stories and finding additional new ways to protect our babies. (Wendy)

- As soon as your baby can reach out and grab things, examine her room for any hanging cords or fragile or dangerous items that she'll be able to reach when she's lying or standing on the changing table, crawling around the floor or standing in the crib.

- As soon as your baby can roll over, cover electrical outlets, tie up long curtain cords, remove dangerous plants and move items that are on the floor that could fall over if your baby bumped them.

- Many babies roll over and over to get where they want to be long before they learn to crawl. As soon as your baby starts trying to roll over, put up safety gates to prevent her from falling down stairs or entering rooms that aren't baby-proof.

- The safest gates to use at the top of stairs are those that bolt into the wall and lock securely. Pressure gates are fine in doorways between rooms.

- To attach a gate to a wall, make sure that you either bolt it into a wood stud or use screws or bolts that are specially-designed for use on plasterboard. If you don't, the gate could rip out of the wall when someone bumps into it or a toddler decides to shake it or climb it.

- When you use a pressure gate, place the locking mechanism on the side away from the room that the baby is in.

- There should never be more than an inch and a half of space between the bottom of the gate and the floor. If there is, your baby could get caught underneath.

- Examine the door stops in your house as soon as your baby is moving around. If the little plastic tip at the end can be removed with little or no effort, take them all off. The coil is less like to hurt a baby than a swallowed plastic tip. It sounds silly, but door stops are at a baby's level, make a great sound when swatted and fit nicely in a little mouth.

- As soon as your baby starts to try to pull up to a stand, remove dangerous items from table tops, put corner guards on table corners, cover the edges of fireplace hearths and put latches on your toilets.

When we first got married and started furnishing our house, Jerry and I decided to get furniture that would be baby proof, easy to clean and practically indestructible since we wanted to have kids soon. I had a coffee table custom-made with rounded corners. As soon as Ben began pulling up, we put edge guards all around the top. One day Ben crawled under the table, lifted his head up and cut his forehead on the bottom edge of the table. I couldn't believe that after all my advance planning, he still got hurt. Now there are edge guards under the table, too. (Jill)

- Cabinet safety locks aren't enough. Move all chemicals, soaps, sponges and other household items that can be harmful to high shelves.

- Closed doors are a wonderful way to keep babies out of the bathroom and other unsafe areas as long as you and everyone else in your house remember to close them. But just in case you don't remember, baby-proof those rooms anyway.

- Door alarms can help you remember to keep doors closed. These alarms sound after a door has been left open ten or fifteen seconds.

- Make sure all television and audio equipment are on safe, sturdy stands.

- You can purchase a hard-to-remove cover that inserts into the opening on your VCR. This protects your baby and your equipment from injury.

- Older homes might not have shatterproof glass in windows or sliding glass doors. Either keep your baby away from these areas, cover the window with a Plexiglas shield, or, if your windows have room for it, place a safety gate in the window frame. Another option, of course, is to replace the windows with safety glass.

- Many homes, newer ones in particular, have very low windows. Either put a safety gate in the window frame to block an open window or use specially-designed window stops to prevent the window from being opened wide enough for a baby to fall out.

- Keep trash cans in locked cabinets or closets. Tie knots in empty plastic bags, such as dry cleaning bags, before throwing them away. Put trash that is particularly dangerous, such as empty bottles from cleaning products and sharp objects, in your outside trash can. Make sure your recycling bins are out of reach, too.

- Long curtain cords can be held up using curtain cord shorteners or cleats. You can also use twist ties from bread bags or garbage bags if you prefer a cost-free solution.

- Even though it's unlikely that your baby could turn on the water and burn himself, make sure the temperature on your water heater is no higher than one hundred and twenty degrees. You're doing a lot of other baby-proofing activities now, you might as well do this, too. It will give you a head start for when your baby turns into a toddler and discovers how to turn on faucets.

- Keep all medications, prescription and over-the-counter, in their original bottles, in a locked container out of reach of even the most adventurous toddler. Not only are you getting things prepared for when your baby is a toddler, but once you have a child, you start to have more people with children over to your house. You don't want someone else's toddler to get into your medicine.

- Sometimes, even when the environment you're in is completely baby-proof, somebody does something that could endanger your baby. Always stay aware of what's going on and how it could affect your baby.

  As her three year-old son rolled the balls across the pool table in my basement, my friend was playing with her baby on the floor. All of a sudden, I realized that if a pool ball bounced off the table, it would fall directly on the baby. I suggested to my friend that she move the baby. Just as the words were coming out of my mouth and she was moving him, a ball flew off the table and landed in the exact spot where he had been. I was very glad I had trusted my instincts and said something— so was my friend. (Cindy)

- It's helpful to get in the habit of surveying any room your baby will be in before you put her down to play. It's easier to baby-proof the room all at once than to jump up to handle unsafe situations as they arise. This is especially important when you're visiting someone else's house. Remember to replace anything you moved before you leave.

- Your home environment also includes your yard. Inspect the plants, fence, deck, and other potential hazards for items that could hurt your baby if he put his mouth or body on them.

- Pools and hottubs are hazards which justify multiple safety precautions. In addition to adequate fencing and well-fitting, locked covers, it's a good idea to have motion sensors that sound an alarm when someone goes in the water. They can be obtained at pool supply stores.

Section Nine

Going Out With Your Baby

Imagine that you've finally gotten the baby ready, dressed yourself, left the house and arrived where you're going. You're thrilled to be out having fun and getting things done. Then something happens. The baby has a messy diaper that leaks all over her, you and everything else. You get to the restaurant and realize you left the diaper bag at home. You get stuck on the highway for hours or worse, get involved in a car accident.

Most of the challenges you'll face when you're out with your baby probably won't even be about the baby. They'll be about whether you've brought what you need, used the baby equipment properly and created a baby-friendly environment wherever you are. Even though we're mothers in an age of convenience—when manufacturers seem to be trying to outdo each other in providing handy, dandy gadgets on every diaper bag, car seat and stroller—it's the planning and preparation that will make the biggest difference in the quality of your experiences out of the house.

CHAPTER TWENTY-SIX

The Logistics of Daily Trips

The days of just grabbing your purse and running out the door are over. Once you're out, you'll find there's a lot more to be aware of and in control of than ever before, too. It's just another fact of motherhood. Your goal now is to create a routine for going out with your baby. There will still be many things to do, but once you get used to the routine, it won't take much thought.

- Get everything you need to take with you packed and in the car. Then feed, burp and change your newborn. The minute you're done taking care of the baby, get into the car and go. If you try to get the baby ready first, before you get everything else ready, you're liable to find that just when you're ready to go, he needs to be changed or fed again.

- Unless the weather conditions are unsafe, it's fine to go out. Dress yourself and the baby appropriately and take whatever special measures are necessary. In some cases this might include heating or cooling the car before you put the baby in. In other situations it might be necessary to cover the car seat or stroller with a blanket so it won't be too hot or cold on your baby's skin.

- Keep a supply of diaper bag items in the same place you keep your diaper bag when you're home. This reminds you to restock the diaper bag, makes restocking easier and cuts down the number of trips back and forth to the baby's room.

I keep a large stock of diapers and wipes in my car. I also keep a small diaper bag in the car. Whenever we go somewhere, I stock the small bag with a minimum of supplies. I know that if I really need to, I can always come out to the car for more. Why carry around so much when extras are easily accessible? I'm always carrying around less than other mothers are, but I know Ridge's patterns well enough to know what I'll need. (Faith)

- Keep extra supplies, such as diapers, baby wipes, water, formula, a blanket and an outfit, in your car for emergencies such as when you forget to restock your diaper bag or when the baby gets diarrhea and quickly uses up everything in the diaper bag. Also keep an extra outfit for yourself in the car. You'll be glad to have it when he gets you messy, too.

- Remember to update the backup supply you keep in the car with larger diapers and clothes as your baby grows.

  One day when we were out running errands, Braden threw up all over himself. I was so proud of myself for keeping an extra outfit in my car for emergencies. My careful planning was finally paying off. Unfortunately, I hadn't planned quite carefully enough. The outfit was way too small for him. Needless to say, that was the end of that outing. We went straight home. (Ellen)

- If you don't have a car, give a lot of thought to how much you should carry with you when you go out. If you have a big budget and you live in a place where you can easily get anything you need, you might want to carry only the essentials. If you can't just buy what you need to handle unexpected situations, you might want to carry some extras with you just in case.

  I love the movie "One Fine Day." Like the mom in the movie, I live in a big city and don't have a car. When I see her pull one thing after another out of the huge bag she carries at all times, it makes me feel better about lugging around extra stuff for those "just in case" moments. Being prepared for almost anything helps me feel in control. (Michelle)

- If you take cans of formula with you, be sure to bring along a can opener.

- Keep empty, re-closeable plastic bags in your diaper bag. They can be used when you need to dispose of a dirty diaper at a friend's house or store dirty clothes, spoons or bibs. The day you don't have one will be the day you need one the most. Make sure to keep the plastic bags in a zippered compartment so your baby can't get to them. While most diaper bags have plastic pouches that are supposedly for the same uses, they often can't be removed for washing. So if you use them once, they're hard to get clean.

  I keep my diaper bag organized by using large re-closeable plastic bags. One bag holds diapers and wipes. Another bag holds Sam's toys. Others hold a change of clothes, snacks, bottles and formula. Not only can I just pull out what I need, but when something leaks, nothing else gets ruined. (Julia)

- Keep a list of emergency phone numbers (doctor, poison control center, relatives, etc.) in your diaper bag. If there's an emergency, you might not be able to quickly remember those numbers. It's also a good idea to put your name and phone number on your diaper bag in case it gets lost.

- It's great to have help when you're getting your baby ready to go out, but even if they're well-intentioned, mothers, friends and even partners don't know your routine. Be extra careful to check everything before you leave the house. Not only should you make sure the diaper bag has diapers, wipes and food in it, but also that it's brought with you. Grandma might be so busy playing with baby, for example, that she forgets that she offered to carry the diaper bag to the car. A well-stocked diaper bag isn't much use if it's left sitting on the counter while you're at the mall. Of course, if this does happen, hopefully you'll have extra diapers, wipes and food in your car or your purse for just such an emergency.

- It might seem easier to carry your baby around in his car seat on busy days, especially if you have a combination car seat/stroller, but it's not best for your baby. You both miss out on a lot of physical contact that you could have by holding him some of the time. Taking him out of the car seat also lets him change his position and his perspective on the world. So, carrying him in your arms or a soft baby carrier or putting him in a stroller might seem harder in theory, but it will probably help him stay happy longer while you're running around getting things done.

- Frequently check your baby's temperature when she's in a cloth carrier on your back or front. The combination of your body heat and the closed space of the carrier can make her overheat quickly.

- Remember to unwrap your baby's blankets, take off his snowsuit or unbutton his sweater when you get inside. Leave the same amount of clothes on him as you have on yourself.

- Sunscreen shouldn't be used on babies under six months of age. Keep your baby fully covered or in the shade until she's six months old.

- If your baby doesn't have much hair, either put a hat on him when he's in the sun or, if he's older than six months, put sunscreen all over his head.

- If a store clerk offers to help you with your bags or packages, let him. You have enough to handle with the baby, the diaper bag, your purse and the stroller or infant car seat.

- If you need help with your purchases, but a store clerk doesn't offer to help, ask. Be sure to tip when appropriate.

- If you put your baby in her infant car seat in the back section of a shopping cart, you don't have much room for your purchases. That's sometimes the only place the car seat fits, however. Many stores have small shopping baskets that fit nicely on the rack underneath the basket. You still might not be able to get a lot at once, but at least the items won't roll off the cart.

- Plastic links are a great way to attach toys to the stroller or car seat. Your baby won't lose his toys and he'll probably like playing with the chain of links, too.

- Another easy way to keep a toy accessible is to thread the seat belt of the stroller through part of the toy.

- It's worth the effort to find stores and restaurants that have chairs in the bathrooms or fitting rooms where you can comfortably nurse your baby. It's also good to know which ones have a diaper changing station or a clean space where you can change your baby's diaper.

A couple of times crouching on the floor and holding Mercer's hands to prevent him from touching anything while I was changing a diaper were

---

What to Try: When Your Baby Hates Being in the Car

BE SURE THE RESTRAINT STRAPS ON THE CAR SEAT ARE ADJUSTED CORRECTLY. If they're too tight, they may be pulling on your baby's shoulders. If they're too loose, she may be sliding around into uncomfortable positions. Read the section on Using the Car Seat Harness on page 186 to make sure you're using the harness safely.

CHECK THE CAR SEAT INSTRUCTIONS to be sure that the car seat is the appropriate model for the size of your baby.

ADJUST THE CAR SEAT. Maybe your baby wants to be more or less reclined, have more or less head support, or have the restraint straps in a slightly different position.

TRY A DIFFERENT CAR SEAT. Borrow one from a trusted friend or ask a store if you can take one out for a test drive. It might be worth getting a new car seat if it makes your baby happier.

PROVIDE A ROLLED UP TOWEL or a specially-designed head rest to support his head or remove the one you're currently using.

ATTACH PICTURES TO THE SEAT in front of her so she has something to look at.

PLAY MUSIC that he likes and sing along.

MAKE A FOOL OF YOURSELF BY MAKING NOISES, funny faces, etc. to distract him until he calms down. The next few times you get into the car, do the same things before he even gets upset. Maybe you can get him in such a good mood that he'll forget to fuss.

enough. I felt like the changing pad and my clothes were filthy from being in the floor of a public restroom. Now I make a conscious effort to go places that have diaper changing stations or large counters in the bathrooms. (Ashley)

- If you can't find a clean, convenient place to change a diaper, you can use the seat of your car. You could try inside the trunk, but it makes me nervous that the trunk could close with the baby inside. Whatever you do, make sure the door can't pinch the baby and that you keep the car keys with you at all times. Don't set them down in the car!

KEEP SPECIAL TOYS IN THE CAR so that she's excited to see them and forgets where she is.

BE SURE THAT HE ISN'T TOO HOT OR TOO COLD, especially if he's in the back seat. Sometimes heat and air conditioning don't make it all the way to where the baby is, so you'll need to leave it on longer and higher than you would for your own comfort. Conversely, maybe the air is blowing on him too hard. Try sitting in the back seat and having someone else drive to see how the temperature and air flow varies in different parts of your car.

SIT NEXT TO HER WHILE SOMEONE ELSE DRIVES or place her car seat in the passenger seat while you drive. Remember that a car seat should never be put in the passenger seat of a car with an activated passenger-side air bag.

MINIMIZE THE AMOUNT OF TIME your baby spends in the car seat when he's not in the car.

USE PLASTIC LINKS TO ATTACH SOFT, SMOOTH TOYS to the car seat so she can always reach them.

PLAN TO TAKE LONG TRIPS DURING NAP times.

REPOSITION THE CAR SEAT in the car so that he can see out the window.

POINT OUT CARS, trucks, airplanes and other exciting sights if your baby is old enough to care and in a position to see out the window.

- No matter how organized you are when going out with your baby, you'll probably want to minimize the number of errands you have to run. Plan your activities so you can get what you need at stores that are close to each other. Shop at a full-service grocery store that sells stamps, has a photo lab, rents videos, cashes checks and provides other necessary services. Bank by mail, phone or direct deposit. Go to dry cleaners, banks, restaurants, drug stores and other establishments with drive-through windows. Shop on-line. Get creative about how you accomplish everything you need to do. Challenge yourself to break old, inconvenient patterns.

- Some kids just hate being in the car. Nothing you do will make them like it any more. If your baby is like this, make more frequent stops and limit your trips to places close to home when you can. But there will just be times when your baby will have to tolerate the situation whether she likes it or not.

> *Catie absolutely screamed every time we put her in the car. We tried moving the car seat, switching car seats and everything else we could think of. We went to great lengths to make car trips as short as possible. Unfortunately, we got into the habit of stopping frequently to let her out to calm down. At one point, when we went on a long trip, we actually set her swing up when we stopped at a rest stop to give her a break. If I had it to do over again, I wouldn't let her think that by crying, she could get us to stop the car. I'd do my best to comfort her, but teach her that she doesn't get out until we get where we are going. Had I done that, I think she would quickly have gotten tired of crying for nothing and learned to handle being in the car.* (Megan)

- Some babies love the car. Consider yourself lucky if yours does. Try not to flaunt it in the face of friends whose babies don't.

- If your ears need to pop when you're driving over a high altitude mountain pass, your baby's probably do, too. Just crying for a little while may be enough to help your baby's ears. If not, give him a bottle or pacifier or stop the car to nurse him.

CHAPTER TWENTY-SEVEN

Safety On Daily Trips

Being Safe in the Car

When all you had to do was buckle your own seat belt and pay attention to the road, the process of staying safe in the car was hardly noticeable. Now there are a lot more steps to getting in and out of the car. You also have a lot more to pay attention to while you're actually driving. The best way to make safety a consistent, yet convenient habit is to develop good car habits from the very beginning. This is an aspect of motherhood that has to be done right the first time and every time.

The majority of car safety issues relate to the proper use of a car seat. To be as safe as possible, you must make sure that the appropriate type of car seat is located safely, installed correctly and fastened properly. No one of these aspects of car seat use is less important than the others. Failure to take care of any of these concerns could lead to tragedy.

In order to make these safety steps effective, though, you must use the car seat every time your baby is in a car. NEVER, NEVER, NEVER UNDER ANY CIRCUMSTANCES allow your baby to be in a moving vehicle without being strapped into a car seat. Babies can be hurt in a parking lot or going around the corner to a friend's house just as easily as on the highway going 55 miles per hour. Never let your baby or child sit on your lap, with or without a seat belt. If your baby is screaming hysterically, stop the car and take care of him. Even if he's sick and you're on the way to the hospital, he must be buckled in a car seat.

USING THE RIGHT CAR SEAT

- The only safe place for a baby in a car is in an approved restraint system. Infant seats, baby carriers and bassinets don't provide any protection.

- Many hospitals, county health departments, Red Cross chapters and automobile insurance companies offer car seat rental programs. Some sell car seats at their discounted cost.

- Never use a car seat that has been involved in a car accident. Microscopic cracks from previous accidents can compromise the seat's ability to protect your baby. This means that you shouldn't buy or borrow a used car seat unless you can trust the owner to tell you the truth about its history.

- Have a rear-facing car seat with you when you leave the hospital. The hospital won't let you take your baby home unless you have one. They might even send someone out to your car to make sure that you're using it.

- *Consumer Reports* has found that using an infant car seat rather than a convertible car seat (one that can also be used facing forward for a toddler) is the safest choice for newborns and small infants.

- If you use a convertible car seat, the overhead shield or T-strap should be at your baby's chest level, not in front of her face. If it isn't in the right place, use a different car seat until your baby is bigger.

- Your baby can use an infant car seat until he's twenty pounds or twenty-six inches long. If your baby reaches one of these measurements before the other, switch him to a toddler car seat, but keep it in the rear-facing position until he's over twenty pounds and twenty-six inches, when he's big enough to sit in the forward-facing position.

- Babies who have just learned to sit sometimes rebel at reclining in an infant car seat. If your baby continually strains forward and is big enough, switch her to a rear-facing convertible car seat. These seats typically put the baby in a more upright position than an infant seat does. Continue to place the car seat facing the rear and in the most reclined position until your baby weighs twenty pounds.

- Don't continue to use an infant car seat once your baby is too big for it. Even though it's convenient to be able to carry the baby around in the infant car seat, it's not as safe for him once he's over the size limit.

- If you have a built-in car seat in your vehicle, be sure to follow the guidelines about the size of child for which it's intended. These seats aren't suitable for babies weighing under twenty pounds.

- If your car is involved in an accident, talk with your insurance agent about whether your insurance company will cover the cost of replacing the car seat.

- If your insurance company won't cover the cost of replacing a car seat which has been involved in a car accident, contact the car seat manufacturer. If you provide an official accident report, some manufacturers will provide a replacement car seat at no cost.

- If you sent in your warranty registration card when you purchased a new car seat, you will receive any recall notices by mail. Car seat recall notices can also be found in baby care and parenting magazines and on bulletin boards at major toy and baby product stores. You can also obtain this information by contacting the U.S. Department of Transportation's Auto Safety Hotline at 800-424-9393. When you call, have your car seat handy so you can provide the necessary information. You can also get information on their web-site, www.NHTSA.DOT.gov.

WHERE TO PUT THE CAR SEAT

- The safest place for a baby is the middle of the back seat. The most convenient place is the front passenger seat, where you can easily reach her. The next most convenient spot is the back seat on the passenger side. You have to weigh the potential risks and benefits of different seat locations for yourself and your baby.

- In addition to safety concerns, the back seat is a good location for the car seat because your baby will become accustomed to it. When he's older, he'll be less likely to feel entitled to sit up front with you.

- Never use a car seat in the front passenger seat of a vehicle with an activated passenger-side airbag. If the bag inflates, it could harm rather than protect your baby.

- If you place a car seat of any type in the front passenger seat, move the seat as far away from the dashboard as possible.

- The base of the car seat should rest firmly and completely on the seat of the car. Some bucket, highly contoured and raised seats aren't safe for use with some car seats.

HOW TO INSTALL THE CAR SEAT

- Read both the instructions that come with your car seat and the instructions that come with your car. If you have any questions about installation, contact the manufacturers of both the car seat and the car.

- Some older cars require supplemental seat belts for use with a car seat. Check your owner's manual. Car dealers typically provide and install these supplemental belts at no charge.

- When you hook the seat belt around the car seat, position the latch so that the release button is facing away from the car seat. If it's not, the car seat could shift and accidentally push the button.

- Use your knee to push down on the car seat while you tighten the seat belt. This will ensure that the belt is tight enough when the weight of the baby pushes the car seat down onto the seat of the car.

- If you can move the car seat from side to side or tilt it forward, the seat belt isn't tight enough.

- Always use a locking clip when you install a car seat with a seat belt that has a sliding buckle, regardless of whether it's a shoulder/lap combination seat belt or just a lap belt. The locking clip keeps the seat belt from loosening. A locking clip should have come with your car seat. Sometimes they are taped or stored on the back of the car seat. If not, you can buy one at a baby or safety products store or through some catalogs.

- The locking clip should be located as close to the seat belt buckle as possible. Put the locking clip on after the seat belt has been tightened. Both the lap belt and the shoulder belt or the excess length from the lap belt must be threaded through the locking clip.

- If your vehicle was manufactured after September 1995, it has at least some seat belts that can restrain a car seat without the use of a locking clip. Check your owner's manual.

- The manufacturer of your car seat can help you determine where it's safe to place and how to safely install your car seat in your particular car.

- If your rear-facing car seat is tilting too far forward, place a folded towel under the front of the base to level it out. Just make sure that the towel is firmly and securely placed so that it won't slide around. At least eighty percent of the base of the car seat should rest directly on the seat of the car.

- If you use an infant seat with a base that stays in the car, always be sure that all the latches attaching the seat to the base have been secured. In some models, it's possible for only one latch to be secured, yet the seat can seem like it's safely attached.

- If your front-facing car seat has a top tether strap but your car doesn't have an anchor for installing it, contact the manufacturer of your car seat or car to get a kit to add one. The car seat manufacturer's toll-free phone number is probably listed on the car seat instructions.

- If you have difficulty installing the car seat or if you just want someone to check and make sure that you did it correctly, contact a local fire station. They will either have people trained to help you or they can refer you to someone who does.

> *My husband and I worried that we might not be installing the car seat properly each time we moved it from one car to the other. We decided to borrow a car-seat from a trusted friend so we had a car seat in each car. It saved us a lot of worrying and a lot of time.* (Brooke)

> *My mother wasn't able to hook the infant car seat into her car very well. Since she picks up Lianne from daycare from time to time, I decided to buy a toddler car seat and install it in her car in the rear-facing position until Lianne is big enough to use it all the time in my car.* (Whitney)

USING THE CAR SEAT HARNESS

- Just having the baby in the car seat isn't nearly enough. He also must be securely buckled in whenever the car is moving.

- The harness straps should be positioned so they come through the slot behind, not above, the baby's shoulders.

- Be sure to follow the manufacturer's instructions for adjusting the height of the shoulder straps. Re-thread, reconnect or tighten the straps exactly as recommended.

- A properly fitting harness allows room for only two fingers between the baby's chest and the harness straps. While a loose fit might seem more comfortable for your baby, it dramatically reduces the safety of the restraint system.

- Blankets should be placed over, not under, the harness. A receiving blanket that's swaddling your newborn is fine, but any more bulk under the straps isn't safe.

- The sliding clip which holds the car seat's harness straps together over the baby's body should be located at chest level. This will prevent your baby from slipping through the straps or from falling too far forward in an accident.

- The harness can protect your baby's life when she's not in the car, too. If you carry your baby around in her car seat, you might as well keep the harness straps attached. Your baby probably won't mind since she'll be used to them, but if you're concerned about her comfort, loosen them or lower the sliding clip while you're not in the car. Just be sure to tighten them again when you put the car seat back in the car.

- Remember to adjust the length of the harness straps after your baby has a growth spurt.

- Keep the manufacturer's instructions with the car seat at all times. Most car seats even have a special compartment to keep them in. That way, they'll be available for reference whenever you switch the car seat from one car to another or want to adjust the seat for your growing baby.

GENERAL CAR SAFETY

- If your baby needs your attention for more than a moment, stop the car and take care of him. Don't try to drive while you help him. Neither activity will get the attention it deserves.

- If you find yourself turning around or adjusting your rearview mirror to see your baby in the back seat, get a mirror designed specifically to help you check on her. One type of mirror attaches easily to your rearview mirror. Another type is placed in the back of your car and lets you see your baby's face while she's in a rear-facing car seat.

- Always keep your keys with you if the baby is in the car. This sounds like an unnecessary reminder, but you have a lot to carry and do when you're getting the baby in or out of the car. It's not uncommon for new mothers to accidentally lock their keys and their babies in the car.

- On hot days, cover the car seat with a blanket or towel when it's not in use so that it doesn't become too hot for the baby to touch when you put him back in the car.

- Only give your baby soft toys while she's in the car. If you stop short or get into an accident, you don't want her face or head to bang into something hard. Be particularly careful about toys, such as toy dashboards, that attach to the car seat.

- Beware of loose items that can become dangerous projectiles if you stop short or get involved in an accident. Keep potentially dangerous objects in closed compartments whenever possible.

- When the car is parallel parked, stand on the curb side when you put the baby in or take him out of the car. It's the safest place for both of you.

- Never leave your baby in the car unattended. Not only could your baby have trouble and need you, but cars have been stolen with babies in them. The convenience of running in to pay for your gas or getting some money out of the ATM without getting the baby out of the car isn't worth the risk of losing your child. Banks with drive-thru windows and gas stations with credit card payment right on the gas pumps are safer and more convenient.

Stroller Safety

Okay, so the potential dangers of a stroller aren't nearly as serious as the risks of not using the car seat properly, but they do exist. You'll probably be using your stroller in public places, where there's lots of activity around you. It's worth keeping the following tips in mind so you can safely pay attention to what's going on around you, not just to the baby.

- Be sure the stroller is completely unfolded and locked in position before you put the baby in.

- Engage the brake when you put your baby in or take him out of the stroller. You don't want the stroller to roll away if it's bumped or placed on uneven ground.

- When you're in a parking lot, place the stroller to the side of the car rather than in front of or behind it. This ensures that passing cars can't run into the stroller and that your car (especially if someone is turning the car on or off while you get the baby situated) doesn't roll into it.

- Always use the safety belt. Even newborns can slide around in a stroller. Older babies can lean over the side on purpose. A fastened safety belt also thwarts anyone who wants to take your baby out of the stroller quickly while you aren't looking.

  Scottie seemed to consider wiggling out of the stroller belt to be a personal challenge from the time he was about eight months old. One day while I was shopping, I heard startled gasps all around me. Scottie had completely toppled over the side of the stroller and was basically doing a headstand next to the stroller. He was thrilled, but I was mortified. I learned to keep a hand on him whenever I was looking at other things. When he was 11 months old, I actually bought a different stroller with a harness instead of a belt. (Regina)

- Avoid overloading the back of your stroller. This will prevent the stroller from tipping over backwards, either with the baby in it or when you remove her.

- If you switch the direction on the stroller handle, be sure to switch the locks on the wheels. These locks control whether or not the wheels can swivel—they're not the "parking" brakes. Whichever direction the handle faces, the wheels closest to you (the back wheels) should be locked and the wheels farthest from you (the front wheels) should be unlocked so you can steer. If all the wheels are unlocked and able to swivel, the stroller will tend to move sideways instead of forward when you push it.

- It's dangerous to push the stroller out from in between parked cars or other large objects because the stroller gets into the street before you have a clear view of any cars that are coming. It's safer for you to walk out first as you pull the stroller behind you.

- Choose store aisles carefully. If they are too narrow, not only could the stroller get stuck, but your baby may be able to reach out and grab the merchandise or get hit in the face with it.

- If you frequently use your stroller at night, put a bicycle reflector on each side of the stroller so it's visible to passing cars.

CHAPTER TWENTY-EIGHT

Eating Out at Restaurants

Eating out with your baby doesn't have to be an activity you reserve for special occasions unless you want it to be. Babies who are taken to restaurants on a regular basis typically tend to do well. Of course, you have to do more than just decide to go out to eat. You also have to select an appropriate restaurant, bring the necessary supplies and time everything carefully so you can have a pleasant dining experience.

- If your baby tends to be very vocal, seek out restaurants that have a higher noise level or outdoor seating.

- If you're unsure whether a restaurant welcomes babies, call and ask whether they have high chairs or if they have certain times when children are allowed. Some finer restaurants, for example, only allow children before six p.m.

- Restaurants are often air conditioned. Bring along a sweater or blanket for the baby in case it's cold or drafty inside, even though it's warm outside.

- If your baby won't be sitting in a high chair, either because she is too young or because she'll be napping or playing instead of eating, you can bring a car seat or stroller in for her. Just be sure to ask for a table that has a lot of space around it. You need room for the stroller or car seat as well as enough space to maneuver around to care for your baby. You don't want to be so close that she can reach out and smear stuff on people at the next table.

- If you want as much privacy as possible so you can nurse, be careful where you sit. Consider the viewpoint of the other diners and of the servers as they come out of the kitchen or stand at the service station.

- It's tempting to ask for a booth if you're nursing, so you won't be so exposed, but some booths are too narrow for comfort. Check it out before you have to wedge your hungry baby in sideways.

- If you use an upside-down wood high chair as a stand for your car seat, be sure that it's stable. If the high chair's seat back is much higher than the front, it may be too unstable to be used upside-down.

- If you use an upside-down wood high chair or a special stand to hold the car seat, position it out of the path of servers. It's also a good idea to keep your foot on one of the rungs to provide added stability.

- If your baby will be sitting in a high chair at the table, always count him as a person when you make reservations or ask for a table. If anything, babies take up more space than an adult or older kid does because you have to move everything on the table out of his reach. Don't say "four and a baby," for example, say "five." Otherwise, you might end up with a high chair pulled up to a table for four. This might be okay if the high chair has its own tray, but if it pulls right up to the table, firmly explain that you need a larger table.

  If I sat down with Matthew on my lap, he protested when it was time to sit in the high chair. If he was put in the high chair right away, it didn't seem to occur to him that there was an alternative. I learned to tell hostesses that we didn't want to be taken to the table until the high chair was already there. (Rosa)

- If you bring baby food or finger foods along with you, select light-colored foods such as applesauce, cereal, bananas or diced potatoes. That way, if your baby makes a mess, it won't show up on either of you as much.

- If your baby tends to be a fussy eater, bring only her favorite foods with you when you go out to eat. You can deal with trying to get her to eat a balanced diet when you're at home.

- If you prefer homemade baby food, but don't like carrying it around with you, bring a food mill with you to the restaurant. Order food your baby can eat, but ask them to leave out spices, seasonings and condiments. There's nothing wrong with grinding up food at the table.

- It's a good idea to bring finger food snacks, such as crackers or dry cereal, with you for your older baby. That way, he won't suffer if the food takes a long time to arrive or if the restaurant doesn't offer a baby-friendly menu.

- Use a diaper wipe to clean the table and high chair before you put your baby into it. Even if the restaurant has cleaned it, the cleaning solution they used probably isn't the safest thing for her hands or food to touch.

- For babies who are just getting used to sitting in a high chair, the wood high chairs that are designed to be pulled up next to the table can be a challenge. Place a rolled jacket, a purse (closed so baby can't reach into it) or a folded blanket behind your baby's back to stabilize him.

- When you use a baby seat that attaches to the table, be sure that it's fastened correctly before seating your baby. Just because the hostess puts them on the table all the time doesn't necessarily mean that she's attaching it correctly. Check it yourself. The seat should be firmly against the edge of table. The arm that goes under the table must be flat against the underside of the table. Attachable seats shouldn't be used for a baby who weighs more than twenty-five pounds.

- It's not safe to use an attachable seat on a glass table, a table top that isn't at least half an inch thick or a pedestal table.

- You shouldn't put the arms of an attachable seat on top of a tablecloth or place mat.

- Don't put a chair under an attachable seat. Instead of protecting your baby from a fall, the chair could actually cause one. If your baby puts her feet on the chair and pushes, she'll take her own body weight off the seat. Since the baby's body weight is what holds the seat on the table, the seat could fall off if she shifts around.

- Get in the habit of asking for crackers, water or anything else you need for the baby as soon as you sit down, not when you order.

- For some reason, perhaps because babies are often positioned at the end of the table, servers have a tendency to hold their trays over the baby's head. Being safe is more important than being polite. Immediately tell the server to move the tray. Then explain the danger.

- Remind servers to place all dishes and items, not just the hot or sharp ones, out of the baby's reach. Since many servers don't realize how far babies can reach, show them where to put things. Give the same reminder to the people with whom you're dining.

- Ice is a great distraction for older babies. It's a readily available, clean and safe plaything. Put a few large pieces on the table and let your baby see how it moves on the table, melts in his hand and is cold in his mouth. When a piece gets small enough that your baby could swallow it, take it away and replace it with a larger one.

- Teach your older baby what you consider "good behavior" in a restaurant, rather than rewarding poor behavior. If the result of misbehavior is the opportunity to sit in your lap or be taken outside, your baby is likely to learn to fuss just to get out of the high chair. If she does fuss, distract her with toys, food or quiet play. If you must take her away from the table, take her to a boring place, such as the rest room, and ignore her as much as possible. Teach her that you're happy to interact with her at the table, but the consequences of fussing aren't fun. This strategy might only have a limited effect now, but it's a good start for when your baby is a toddler.

Leo and I know that we can't expect Jessica to sit still in the high chair from the time we arrive to the time we leave. We either hold her in our lap or walk around outside with her until the food comes. When the food is there, though, we expect her to sit in the high chair. Once in a while she fusses, but not often. (Sandy)

After several occasions when Noah threw his toys so hard that they landed on other people's tables, we learned to bring a special set of toys with us to restaurants. They either have a suction cup that attaches to the table or they can be attached with links to the high chair. (Margaret)

- Some older babies behave best if they can eat right away. Then they can play or have dessert while the adults eat. Other babies, typically ones who self-feed well, do better if they can talk, play and be entertained in their high chair before the meal is served, then eat while the adults are eating. You'll just have to experiment to find out what works best for your family.

- When you order food for your baby, be sure to tell the waitress whether you want it to come as soon as possible or when your food arrives.

- If your baby makes a huge mess on the floor, pick up the big pieces that a carpet sweeper can't handle, apologize and leave a generous tip. You're not expected to clean up everything, but picking up some of the mess will help you avoid dirty looks from fellow patrons and restaurant staff.

Section Ten

Traveling With Your Baby

Going to wonderful places is no fun if you're stressed and exhausted because of a fussy baby. It's miserable to come home from a vacation more tired and frustrated than when you left. But avoiding travel just because you have a baby certainly isn't the answer. That will only make you feel resentful, bored and lonely. As with daily trips out of the house, planning is the key to success for overnight travel.

Your focus should be on the traveling itself and the time you'll spend in the hotel room or someone else's house. This is what tends to get complicated, not the part about planning all the fun activities you'll do and the people you'll visit. During her first year, your baby will probably be happy to tag along with whatever you do—assuming you're not into skydiving, marathon running, rock climbing or other extreme activities. When you have everything you need to make sure that your baby can eat, sleep and play as normally as possible, you're much more likely to have an enjoyable time. When your baby is happy and relaxed, you can be, too.

CHAPTER TWENTY-NINE

Planning What to Bring

Babies need a lot of stuff, but they don't need everything all of the time. So, to reduce the hassle of packing and carrying all that stuff when you travel, you have to decide exactly what you'll need while you're away. You also have to evaluate whether you can easily get what you need where you're going or if you need to bring it with you.

Personally, I'd rather inconvenience myself by bringing a bit too much than get into a situation when I don't have something I need. I'm convinced that if you bring the critical pieces of baby paraphernalia, stay calm and maintain your regular routines as much as possible once you're there, everything will probably turn out just fine.

- There are two easy ways to make sure that you pack everything you need for the baby. One is to put each item that you use during a full day into a pile immediately after you use it. The other is to list each item as you use it. Then, once you've handled the items you use on a daily basis, you need to consider unexpected events such as a dramatic change in weather or your baby getting sick.

- Packing by category is another way to help you remember everything. The general categories and samples of items you need to remember include:

  DIAPERING (diapers, wipes, empty plastic bags for disposal, ointment)

  DRESSING (clothes for a variety of temperatures and occasions)

FEEDING (breast pump, formula, bottle supplies, food, baby utensils, bibs, storage containers, sippy cups)

BATHING (bath toys, baby soap, bath seat)

ENTERTAINMENT (favorite, but replaceable toys and books, tape recorder and tapes, videos)

SECURITY ITEM(S) (pacifier, favorite blanket, special stuffed animal)

SLEEPING (travel bed, sheet, pajamas)

SAFETY (outlet covers, curtain ties, safety gate)

HEALTH (prescription medications, over-the-counter remedies in case of cold or fever, thermometer, humidifier)

CAR (car seat, tapes or CD's, car toys)

> *We got so frustrated with trying to fit all of Billy's stuff into the trunk of the car that we rented a minivan for our vacation.* (Anna)

> *I learned to choose what to bring based on where we were going. When we visit my parents in a small town where stores close early and don't carry a wide variety of items, I brought enough supplies for the whole trip. I also brought emergency supplies such as over-the-counter medicines. If we went to visit friends in a suburb of a major city, I had easy access to a 24-hour grocery store. I only brought what I needed while we were traveling, then I went shopping to get what I needed while I was there. I didn't bring emergency supplies because I knew I could easily get them if and when I needed them.* (Chelsea)

- You don't need full-size containers of each and every type of supply. You can either buy travel-sized containers or transfer what you need into re-closeable plastic bags or small plastic Tupperware®-type containers. The only item that shouldn't be transferred into a different container is medicine of any kind.

- When your baby will be sleeping in an unfamiliar place, bring familiar items such as crib toys, music and blankets. If he can look at the same toy that he always looks at before falling asleep, for example, the fact that he's in a different room may not matter.

- Bring one of your baby's crib sheets with you when you travel. Not only will it smell and feel like home, but, if you're staying at a hotel, she won't have to put her face on something washed in harsh, industrial-strength detergents.

- Bring outlet covers, cord ties and removable cabinet locks with you. This makes staying in a hotel room, condo or someone's house significantly less stressful and much more safe.

  My husband always goes in to evaluate the hotel room while Courtney and I wait in the car with all our stuff. It's a lot easier to change rooms before we start unloading. (Martha)

  Steve and I like to stay in unusual places when we travel. The first time we traveled with Rose, we made reservations at a place that had cabins instead of rooms. Unfortunately, they were so small there wasn't enough room to set up the travel bed. From then on, we've stayed only at large chain hotels when we travel with the baby. What we lose in creativity is more than made up for by what we gain in consistency. (Marina)

- If you're staying at the home of someone who has children, discuss the equipment you need to bring. They may still have some baby spoons, sippy cups, a playpen or a high chair. Just make sure to check that these items are still safe and clean for your baby's use.

- If you frequently stay in a particular place, such as your mother's house or your condo in the mountains, it might be easier to get a set of supplies and equipment to leave there instead of carrying it with you all the time. Just be sure to check expiration dates on supplies such as formula and medicine on a regular basis. Also remember to leave larger sizes of clothing as your baby grows.

- Many hotels are happy to provide you with a crib, high chair and small refrigerator in your room. All you have to do is ask. It's best to make these arrangements before you arrive, however, so that if these items aren't available you can plan accordingly.

- You can rent baby items such as car seats, strollers, cribs, rocking chairs, soft baby carriers, swings, high chairs, back-packs and breast pumping equipment as an alternative to bringing everything with you. Even items such as toys and videotapes may be available. Look under "Rental" in the yellow pages or call directory assistance for the area you will be visiting. Car seats can also be rented from car rental companies.

- If you rent equipment, be as careful in your selection as you would be if you were purchasing it. Make sure each item is Juvenile Products Manufacturer's Association (JPMA) certified and is free of potentially dangerous defects or damage. Cleanliness is another factor to consider. Don't be shy about asking for a different piece of equipment if necessary. You are purchasing a service, not asking for a favor. You should be completely confident of the quality of the products you rent.

- If you need large safety items such as safety gates or just prefer not to bring all your safety equipment with you, some of these baby-oriented rental companies also offer baby-proofing services in some major resort and vacation locations.

- When you pack for a trip, make sure to pay attention to what you bring for yourself. With all that you have to do, it's easy to focus so much on packing back-up clothes and emergency supplies for the baby that you forget the most basic necessities for yourself.

- In can be tempting to try to bring as little for yourself as possible since the baby's stroller, travel bed, car seat and other equipment are so large and heavy. Just remember that you have so much to carry that a slightly larger bag for you, or even an extra bag altogether, may not make that significant a difference.

- One of the most helpful things you can bring with you on a trip is a baby-sitter. If you have a trustworthy teen-ager with you, you'll have an extra pair of hands as well as someone to stay with the baby while you enjoy adult activities.

CHAPTER THIRTY

Adapting to the Place You're Staying

Concerns to Handle Before You Leave Home

It's a good idea to find out about the amenities, routines and logistics of the place you'll be staying before you leave. The better informed you are, the easier it will be to ensure that you'll be in a baby-friendly environment. It will also be easier to adjust once you get there. Talking with people at your destination will also help them prepare so you and your baby are as safe and comfortable as possible and cause minimal disruption.

- If you're worried about how your baby will sleep away from home, go on a few test runs to help both of you get used to the idea before you go. Let him nap in his travel bed or in a crib at a friend's house to help him become familiar with sleeping somewhere other than his own room and crib.

- Safety concerns are a particular issue if you will be staying in an apartment or townhouse style condo instead of a traditional hotel room. There may be stairs, balconies and other amenities that are unsafe for mobile babies. Your best bet is to specify your room preferences when you make reservations. Then, just to double check, call a few days before you'll be arriving and ask for a specific description of the particular unit you'll be using. If the unit you're given isn't satisfactory, ask for another. If the staff is reluctant to move you, remind them that having an injured baby will be a much bigger problem than shuffling room assignments.

- If your baby crawls or walks and you'll be staying in someone's home, have a discussion with them about safety issues before you arrive. Describe the baby's physical abilities and mobility level. Ask them whether you need to bring a gate, outlet covers or other safety equipment. Ask them whether they're willing to move dangerous items, such as cleaning supplies, houseplants and large, unstable objects before you arrive. Explain that it would be helpful to have at least one area in which the baby can safely move around, under your supervision of course.

- If your host doesn't want to make any changes to the house to accommodate your safety concerns, plan to spend some of your time away from the house. It's no vacation to spend the whole time chasing your baby around the house, snatching things out of her hands, holding your breath that nothing will break and constantly saying, "don't touch."

- It's also appropriate to discuss household routines and rules with your host. It will be helpful to know what times they usually eat, when they wake up in the morning and whether they allow snacks in the family room, for example. If their habits are consistent with yours, you can anticipate a relaxing visit. If they're not, you need to do a little planning to determine how you will adjust your ways to meet your baby's needs in a manner that works with their household. If you're concerned that your baby tends to be fussy in the morning, for example, ask them to put you in the most soundproof room or offer to go out to breakfast as soon as the baby wakes up.

- Let the people you're visiting know your baby's schedule in advance. The more they know up front, the easier it will be to make appropriate plans.

Handling Situations That Arise While You're There

Even if you've brought everything you could possibly need, your baby may behave differently when you stay somewhere other than home.

You're likely to find that you behave differently, too, since you have to consider other people's preferences, schedules and lifestyles as well as your own. If you're not careful, the stress and frustration of traveling with a baby could leave you feeling as if you need a vacation, not as if you just had one!

- It's natural to want your baby to be on her best behavior when you're with other people. Just make sure that you don't get so stressed about it that your stress rubs off onto her. Think about how hard it must be for her to behave properly in a new situation.

- If you're staying with people who seem to want to help you take care of your baby, let them! They'll probably enjoy it. Sometimes you can be with them while they keep busy with the baby. Maybe there will be other times when they'll give you a complete break from baby care.

- Try not to plan on too many activities. It won't do you any good to let your baby get over-tired or over-stimulated. You might have fun that day, but the next will be miserable.

- You have every right to be firm about what will and won't work for your family. It's hard to disappoint people when they want to have fun with you, but you have to explain that certain activities won't be fun if the baby is tired and fussy.

- Make sure to take some time alone with your baby. It will help both of you relax. It will also help you maintain some semblance of normalcy.

- You and your partner should discuss how you'll share the baby care responsibilities while you're away. It's no fair for you to be the only one who stays behind while the baby naps or while everyone else is doing activities that aren't baby-friendly. Take turns so both of you can have some real vacation time.

- Dramatic transitions in altitude can cause major behavioral changes in your baby. If you go from low to high altitude, for example, ear pressure may cause your baby to nurse or bottle-feed less vigorously or frequently. Going from high to low altitudes may give your baby (and you) a headache and make him feel fussy or lethargic. Plan on a few days of adjustment to the new environment. Keep your schedule as normal and stress-free as possible during this period.

- If you'll be traveling to a different time zone, you have to evaluate how long you'll be there, how many hours difference there are and how well your baby adapts to changes in her schedule to determine whether or not you should try to shift her to the new time zone. If the change is only a couple of hours, it might be easiest just to keep her on the old time zone. If the change is significant or your stay will be an extended one, you can help her adjust. During the first day or so, keep her normal schedule for the time it is at home. Then gradually start moving her feeding and sleeping times to the new hours. Do the reverse when you return home.

CHAPTER THIRTY-ONE

Traveling by Plane

The process of getting ready to travel by plane isn't much different than preparing to travel by car, but the stakes tend to feel a little higher. You can't get into your bags or equipment any time you want, your baby may be in your lap instead of in a car seat, there's a limit to how much you can bring with you, you have to conform to someone else's schedule and there's an inherent lack of control which can stress you out. You can't change the logistics of airplane travel, but preparing well will help you have the time, energy and appropriate supplies to make a big impact on the most critical factor in having a pleasant, low-stress flight—your baby's mood.

Making Reservations

- When you make a reservation, let the airline know you'll be traveling with an infant so they'll list him on the flight manifest.

- Plan your travel time around your baby's schedule and temperament. If she can't sleep anywhere but her own crib, try to travel during the time when she's usually awake. If your baby is very active, plan to fly during nap or nighttime. The excitement and tension of the trip might throw your baby off her normal schedule or behavior, but it's worth a try.

    Stephanie does best if we fly at night. The plane is darker and quieter, so she sleeps most of the time. (Frannie)

- Ask for a flight that tends not to be full. Not only will you have more room for stuff, but you might even end up with a free empty seat for the baby.

- If you don't plan on booking a seat for your baby, ask for a seat or seats next to an empty seat. Hopefully that seat will stay empty so you can use it. If you book your seats in advance and both parents are traveling with the baby, book two seats that have an empty seat between them. Middle seats are the last to be assigned by the airline. If someone does get seated in the middle seat, however, there's no doubt that he or she will be happy to exchange either with one of you or with someone else who will allow you to sit together.

- If you plan to keep your baby in a car seat on the plane, ask the airline if they require that the car seat be approved for use on an airplane. A sticker on the side of the car seat will indicate if it's airline approved.

- Get seats close to the front of the plane so you can get off as quickly as possible.

- When you check in at the airport, ask if the bulkhead seats are available. These seats typically aren't assigned in advance, but, if they're available, they'll provide you with much needed extra space.

Preparing for the Flight

- If you even suspect that your baby might have an ear infection, check with the pediatrician before traveling by plane. The changes in air pressure can damage fluid-filled ears.

- Take extras of everything in your carry-on bag. Have a change of clothes for you and the baby and enough food and diapers to last at least a day. Carry any prescription medications as well as fever and cold remedies with you. Should you get stuck in the airport overnight or have to make an unscheduled stop somewhere, it will have been worth the effort to lug all that stuff around.

- Airports are not safe places. Never, never take your eyes off your baby. Don't leave her in the stroller outside the stall in the bathroom. Don't leave her in the stroller or car seat behind while you check in at the desk. Don't ask someone else to watch her for a moment.

- When you pass through airport security, you'll have to take the baby out of the stroller or car seat. Plan accordingly.

- If you don't want to bring a stroller or you prefer to check it with your luggage, a soft baby carrier or backpack can be a convenient alternative that leaves your hands relatively free while you're in the airport.

  I found that it was easiest to use a front carrier when I was traveling alone with Rebecca. I could even go to the bathroom with her in it. (Maria)

- Gate check large items, such as a stroller or car seat, that you need immediately before and after the flight. Check in at the counter at the gate and have the item tagged for gate check. Take the item to the end of the jetway and leave it just before you get on the plane. This absolutely ensures that these items will be on the same plane you're on. In some cases, the items will be waiting for you on the jetway when you get off the plane. Otherwise, they'll go to baggage claim.

  We travel so much that we bought an inexpensive stroller that folds up like an umbrella. It fits in the overhead compartments of most planes, it isn't the end of the world if it gets dirty or lost, and it's easy to pick up and carry if we need to. It was just too hard to deal with our big, beautiful stroller during a trip. (Erica)

- Don't get so busy caring for your baby that you forget to care for yourself. Eat something and go to the bathroom before you board. A flight is much more enjoyable if you don't have to eat while you're holding your baby or endure him pressing on your full bladder as he sits in your lap.

- I think it's best to save the baby's sleep time for on the plane. If possible, try to keep her awake while you're in the airport, at least until you're just about to board the plane.

Managing on the Plane

- You, your baby and anyone else traveling with you should wear comfortable clothes and shoes that are easy to clean. Forget about fashion. No matter what you wear, you'll probably be somewhat disheveled when you get off the plane. You might as well be comfortable.

- Change your baby's diaper just before you get on the plane so you can avoid one of the most difficult aspects of plane travel—changing a baby's diaper in the lavatory. Very few planes are equipped with enough space in which to lay your baby down, let alone a real changing table. So, unless your baby has an offensive diaper or you're on an extremely long flight, wait until you get off the plane.

> *During my last flight with Shayna, she behaved beautifully, but she had an upset stomach. There was no question that her diaper needed to be changed. The only issue was where to do it. With everyone waiting in line, I couldn't do it on the floor in front of the bathrooms. It was too messy to try to change on a seat. The flight attendants were adamant that I couldn't change her on the floor of the galley. So I had to do the best I could in the lavatory. By laying her across the sink part of the time and having her stand up on the counter the rest of the time, I was able to manage. If that hadn't worked, I was considering just sitting her down in the sink and rinsing her off.* (Lori)

- If you're concerned that your baby will be restless on the plane, don't board until the last minute. If two adults are traveling with the baby, one of you can get on early to stow your carry-on items while the other one waits with the baby until final boarding is called. Since most planes don't take off when they're actually scheduled, this may save you up to half an hour of time just sitting on the plane.

- Take out a bottle, toys, wipes, and anything else you might need in the first few minutes of the flight and put them on the seat next to you or in the seatback pocket before the plane takes off. It's next to impossible to hold a baby, lean over and dig through a diaper bag while the plane is going up and your baby is fussing.

- If you purchased a seat for your baby or are lucky enough to get an empty seat next to you, you can use a car seat on the plane. Install the car seat just like you would in the car, except you don't need to use the locking clip. Make sure to position the belt buckle so the latch can't accidentally be pushed up and released by the car seat or the baby.

- If your very young or small baby gets restless or annoyed at being held, let him sit or lie down on the tray. Never let go of him and always make sure your knees are right under the tray to support the weight of the baby. The trays aren't strong enough to hold anything but a very small infant.

- If your baby is sitting on your lap, ask the person seated in front of you to notify you before he or she reclines the seat. Otherwise, the seat could bump your baby on the head. Hopefully, this gentle reminder will encourage the other passenger to keep the seat back in its upright position.

- Changes in altitude affect a baby's ears as much as they affect yours. Make sure your baby drinks or sucks on something whenever your ears feel like they need to pop. She doesn't need to suck from the minute you start to take off until you level off or from the time descent begins until you land.

- Stay alert when other passengers are loading or unloading their belongings from the overhead bins and when food trays are being passed. You don't want anything to fall on or bump into your baby.

- If you're sitting on the aisle, be extra vigilant when the flight attendants are doing drink or meal service. If your baby's hands, feet or head extend into the aisle even a little bit, they could get bumped by the food cart.

- When drinks are being passed out, ask for an unopened can of apple juice for your older baby. It never hurts to have an extra supply.

- If you're holding a baby in your lap, it can be extremely difficult to keep your tray in place, your baby's hands out of the food and your drink right-side up. So, if you're traveling alone, your best bet is to eat before you get on the plane and pass on the full meal. You can also ask if there's something on the tray you can hold in your hand to eat, such as a piece of fruit or a muffin.

    *I always bring a sandwich for myself and food and snacks for my baby
    with me. That way we can eat whenever we're hungry and don't have*

to rely on the airline's schedule. I also like having something that's easy to eat while I'm holding Nathan. (Ruby)

- If you're traveling with someone else, take turns eating. Just ask the flight attendant to hold the other meal until you're ready.

- Choose a cold meal if you have an option. Spilled food isn't such a big deal if it isn't hot.

- Be as considerate as you can of other passengers, but don't let them make you feel guilty. People who haven't done it have no idea how hard it is to travel with a baby. People who have done it will understand completely.

Finding and Using Baby-Sitters

Few situations will make you feel more like an adult and a real mother than finding someone trustworthy to baby-sit for you. As you explain how to care for your baby, you'll suddenly realize how much you know about your baby's patterns and how many responsibilities you handle. At first it may feel strange to relinquish those duties for a while. You're probably so used to being with your baby that it might be difficult to totally relax while you're away. Don't worry, though. As you develop a list of dependable sitters and get used to providing the necessary instructions before you leave, you'll be able to take full advantage of your brief periods of freedom.

CHAPTER THIRTY-TWO

Finding Baby-Sitters

There are two steps to finding baby-sitters. The first is developing a list of trustworthy people who tend to be available during the times you'll usually need them. The second is finding a sitter from that list for a specific date and time when you want to go out. Both activities tend to take a lot of time and effort. Both will be done repeatedly until your children are old enough to stay home alone. You might as well get good at it now.

What to Try: To Find Baby-Sitters

Use the following resources to find baby-sitters:

NEIGHBORS and neighborhood directories

FRIENDS

FAMILY MEMBERS

COMMUNITY BULLETIN BOARDS (at community centers, grocery stores, local schools, places of worship, etc.)

DOCTORS' OFFICES (yours and your baby's)

SERVERS AT RESTAURANTS, clerks at stores, etc. who seem to be good with babies

BABY-SITTERS YOU ALREADY USE (ask them to suggest a friend when they aren't available to baby-sit)

I didn't know anyone in my new neighborhood, so I took lots of walks with Micah in his stroller. I went out of my way to talk to people who were in their yards, especially if they were teen-agers. It didn't take long to find a few baby-sitters. (Debbie)

• Some people jealously guard their list of baby-sitters, refusing to give out any names. Don't be surprised if some of your neighbors don't want to share.

• Once you've found a potential baby-sitter, ask her the following questions:

❏ How long have you been baby-sitting?

❏ What age children have you taken care of?

❏ Have you taken a baby-sitting class?

❏ Are you familiar with infant CPR and techniques to help a choking baby?

❏ Will your mother or father be home when you're baby-sitting?

❏ What days of the week and during what hours can you baby-sit?

❏ Have you baby-sat for anyone else in the neighborhood that I might know?

❏ Is there anything that you're uncomfortable doing or unsure of how to handle with children the age of my child?

❏ What do you charge?

• Teen-aged baby-sitters often find it awkward to answer the question, "What do you charge?" Don't be surprised if a baby-sitter says she'll take whatever you want to give her. An easier way to handle the issue is to find out the going rates from your neighbors, then ask the sitter if that's okay with her.

- Don't be afraid to consider twelve and thirteen year-old baby-sitters. As long as you've met them and are comfortable that they're mature enough to care for your child, the benefits include:

  ❏ They can't drive and probably don't have friends who can, so you don't need to worry about them leaving or having friends come over.

  ❏ They tend to be too young to have boyfriends so they won't have boys over or spend lots of time on the phone talking with them.

  ❏ They tend to be young enough to find baby-sitting a thrill and are honored to be trusted.

  ❏ They take their responsibility seriously and tend to know their limits and capabilities.

  ❏ They follow, rather than question, your instructions.

  ❏ They enjoy playing with babies.

  ❏ Their social schedule is not yet very busy with dating and dances, which would tend to rule out Friday and Saturday availability.

  ❏ Their mothers and fathers tend to be fairly involved in their schedules, approving baby-sitting dates and ensuring that they arrive on time.

  ❏ You can continue to use them for years to come.

- The biggest problem with younger baby-sitters is that some aren't available on school nights or can't stay out late. This shows that they have responsible, caring parents, which isn't a drawback, of course. This is only a "problem" in terms of your ability to use them as baby-sitters.

  I use older baby-sitters when I'll be away during a mealtime. I'm not comfortable with a twelve or thirteen year-old feeding Juliana, but they're fine to play with her, change a diaper and put her down for a nap. (Eva)

- If a teen-aged boy seems interested and able, there's nothing wrong with using him as a baby-sitter. Check out his qualifications just as you would any other potential baby-sitter.

- Unless you have your own private crew of baby-sitters who are always on call for you, plan on making a few phone calls each time you need to schedule a baby-sitter. Between answering machines and baby-sitters having to check with their parents before they confirm a baby-sitting date, you might have to make quite a few calls.

- When you leave a message for a baby-sitter regarding a baby-sitting date, be specific about the day, time and length of time that you'll need her. This might save a few phone calls back and forth.

- Don't be afraid to leave messages on several baby-sitters' answering machines. The baby-sitter who calls back first gets the job. When the others call back, try to schedule other baby-sitting dates with them.

- Another trick to make scheduling baby-sitting dates easier is to schedule another baby-sitting date each time a baby-sitter is at your house. If you like to go out frequently, try not to let a sitter leave your house without another time planned.

  I've found that it's easier to call baby-sitters and set up several baby-sitting dates for the next month or six weeks with each one. Then, when we have things we want to do or places we want to go, we schedule them into the nights when we already have baby-sitters lined up. This is much easier than frantically trying to find a baby-sitter for a certain evening. (Hedy)

- If scheduling is still a problem, consider hiring a baby-sitter to come on a regular basis. This makes scheduling the baby-sitter and planning your activities a lot easier.

  I got so sick of trying to find baby-sitters when I needed them that I started scheduling my activities around them. I have one sitter who comes every other Friday night and another one who comes on the second Saturday of each month. I try to fit everything I want to do into those evenings. (Mary)

- If you have a lot of difficulty finding teen-aged baby-sitters or you're more comfortable leaving your baby with an adult, trade baby-sitting with a friend. Make sure you work out the agreement for trading first, though. Do you only count how much time overall or is there a premium on certain times? Is it an even trade if you have one baby and she has two kids? Can you call on the spur of the moment or is advanced planning necessary?

- Some neighborhoods have baby-sitting co-ops that give parents a formal system for keeping track of how much time they spend taking care of other kids and how much baby-sitting time is owed to them. If your neighborhood doesn't have one, maybe you can start one. It's a great way to get some time off as well as to meet other moms and kids in your neighborhood.

- Another way to find older baby-sitters is to put a notice up on the job board at a local college.

CHAPTER THIRTY-THREE

Using Baby-Sitters

Dealing with a baby-sitter is like dealing with an employee. First, you need to feel confident of your right to instruct her on how you want the job performed. Then you need to give her the information she needs to do the job well. Once she's working for you, you need to monitor her performance, acknowledge her positive efforts, then either assist her to correct any areas needing improvement or stop using her. It pays to take these responsibilities seriously. Your peace of mind and convenience as well as your baby's well-being are at stake.

- Before you leave your baby with a new baby-sitter, ask her to come over for an hour or so while you're home. Let her observe as you feed, change and play with your baby for a while. Then let her try. You don't need to be with her every minute, though. Use this time to do things around the house. Just listen and casually observe her ability to both care for and play with your baby. If your baby starts to fuss, let her try to handle it. That could be your best indication of her baby-sitting abilities. Step in only to clarify your instructions, show her how to do something you didn't previously address or take over if she seems in over her head. Pay her just as you would if you weren't home.

- Dependability is an extremely important asset in a baby-sitter. If someone doesn't show up or shows up late on a regular basis, you probably don't want to use her anymore. If you don't want to stop using her altogether, you can use her only when your plans aren't time sensitive. If you want to make sure she comes at all, make sure to call to confirm each baby-sitting date with her.

219

After several occasions when a baby-sitter forgot to come, I learned to confirm each date a couple of days in advance, especially if it's for a Friday or Saturday night. I also like to make sure that her parents know her baby-sitting schedule so they can remind her. (GeeGee)

- The baby-sitter doesn't have to come at exactly the time you need to leave. If you want some time to relax and get ready, schedule her to come a bit earlier. Not only will this be nice for you, but it may make it easier for your baby to see you go, since he'll already be involved with the baby-sitter by the time you leave.

  I have a baby-sitter who does a great job with Johnny. She's reliable, except she often arrives a few minutes late. I've solved the problem by scheduling her to come 15 minutes before I actually need to leave. (Brandi)

- If you're fortunate enough to have family members who are willing to baby-sit for you, don't abuse the privilege. Never assume that they're available whenever you want them. Ask them whether they're available on certain dates rather than informing them of your schedule. It's still a good idea to have other baby-sitters so that family members don't begin to feel taken advantage of. You'll also have added flexibility if they're unavailable when you need them.

- If you ask a family member to baby-sit, it's also important to clarify their expectations about payment. If it's a twenty year-old niece, you probably should offer. If it's your mother and she baby-sits on a regular basis, maybe you should occasionally bring her a gift or take her out for a nice meal to express your appreciation. If you're not sure what's appropriate, discuss it with her. She'll appreciate your consideration.

- When you're going out with friends who have children, consider sharing a baby-sitter at one of your houses. If there are a lot of kids, ask your baby-sitter to bring a friend to help. Make it clear to both sitters that their job is to care for the children, not to have fun with each other. The total amount paid to the sitters should be enough that each baby-sitter receives her normal fee for the time she spent baby-sitting, plus a tip. The parents then split the total amount paid according to how many children they're paying for. This will probably end up being less expensive than hiring a baby-sitter on your own.

Information to Leave for a Baby-Sitter

YOUR CHILD'S VITAL INFO, including name, birthdate, allergies and health status.

YOUR HOME PHONE NUMBER, address and closest major cross streets.

THE BABY'S DOCTOR'S PHONE number.

PHONE NUMBERS OF FRIENDS OR FAMILY members who can be called in an emergency.

WHERE YOU'LL BE, including the address and phone number, being as specific as possible. For example, tell her the name of the meeting or party, not just the name of the hotel in which it's being held.

WHAT TIME YOU'LL BE BACK.

LOCATION OF FIRE EXTINGUISHERS and other emergency equipment and exits.

I programmed important phone numbers into the speed dial on my home phone. A large, easy-to-read note with all the speed dial codes is posted right next to the phone. When a baby-sitter arrives I show her the sign and teach her how to use my phone. (Joelle)

- Pagers and cellular phones can really help you increase your freedom and spontaneity when you go out since your sitter can reach you no matter where you decide to go. If you don't already have one, it might be worth it to get one so you can feel more relaxed when you're out. Just be sure to stay within the activated zone of your pager or cellular phone when you use it.

- If you plan to go to the movies, make sure to leave the office phone number of the theater. The number listed in the phone book or the newspaper is usually a pre-recorded movie hotline. To obtain the office number, call directory assistance or ask for the number when you arrive at the theater, then call home to give the number to the baby-sitter. Also tell her the name of the movie you'll be watching.

- Even if your baby-sitter is an adult relative, make sure to provide the same information you would for a teen-aged sitter.

- This may seem obvious, but if you don't want the baby-sitter to leave the house, with or without the baby, tell her. Baby-sitters have been known to run across the street to get something from their house while

Instructions to Discuss with Baby-Sitters

This is great information to go over the first time a new sitter comes, when it's been a long time since the sitter took care of your baby and when your baby has recently had significant developmental advances. The list is long, so you might want to leave written instructions about particularly important topics.

FEEDING
what time
what food/drink
how much
how to prepare a bottle
does the bottle or food need to be warmed
how should it be warmed
how long should it be warmed
where does the baby eat
what assistance does the baby need
what cup should be used
how to clean up the baby

SLEEPING
what time
where
does the baby need to be changed into pajamas
where are the pajamas
does the baby need to be placed in a certain position
does he need to be covered with a blanket
what should and shouldn't be in the crib
should the bedroom door be open or closed
should a night light be on

the baby is napping, have a friend come watch the baby while they leave with a boyfriend or take the baby out for a quick trip to the mall.

I use a fool-proof method to ensure the safety of my baby and baby-sitter and to make sure that the baby-sitter doesn't invite friends over—put on the alarm as I leave the house. If the baby-sitter opens the door, the alarm goes off. Just before I leave, I remind the sitter what will happen if the door is opened. I also show her the panic button on the alarm so that if she needs help, she knows how to get it. (Marjorie)

I keep a list of my rules and instructions for baby-sitters on my computer. Whenever anything changes I can make a quick update. I like

THE BABY'S SAFETY

what are the baby's abilities (roll over, crawl, pull up, etc.)

what rooms are unsafe for the baby

where the baby can be placed (swing, playpen, crib, etc.) while the baby-sitter is on the phone, in the bathroom, preparing a bottle, etc.

where he can't be placed (counter, sofa, bed, etc.)

THE BABY'S BEHAVIOR

how to tell when he's hungry, tired, wet, etc.

the baby's favorite toys

ways to amuse him

the baby's crying patterns

if he's colicky, how he acts

what to do to comfort the baby

THE SITTER'S SAFETY

rules for answering the door (for example, never open the door)

rules for answering the phone (for example, say that you're unable to come to the phone instead of saying that you're not home)

HOUSEHOLD RULES

can she make personal calls (other than to her parents)

can she cook

what can she eat and drink

can friends visit

can she smoke in the house

my sitters to have written instructions so there's no doubt in their minds about what is and isn't okay. (Bette)

- If a baby-sitter will be at your home during a mealtime, either prepare something for her or tell her what foods are available for her to eat. Be explicit so there aren't any misunderstandings.

The first and only time I used a particular thirteen year-old, I explained everything about taking care of Joanna, but I wasn't specific about my household rules. When I asked if she had eaten dinner, she said that she had. Just in case, I explained to her what food was available if she decided she was hungry. When I came home there was an empty pizza box on the counter. I was furious that she let a pizza delivery man in the house. However, I partly blame myself for not explaining that I didn't want the door opened for anyone. (Heidi)

- The first time you use a new baby-sitter, go somewhere close to home so you can return quickly if you're needed. Then come home a little bit earlier than you said you would. This will allow you to see how the baby-sitter is doing when she's not expecting you to walk through the door any minute. It may also relieve some of your nervousness to know you're close by in case of an emergency.

- Unless your baby-sitter sees your baby on a daily basis, remind her each time she comes about your baby's new abilities and interests. She might not realize that what was inaccessible for your baby last week is now well within reach. Be explicit.

- Each time they come, remind your sitters that they can never leave the baby unattended on a bed, couch or changing table—even for a second.

    I tell baby-sitters to change and dress Rachel on the floor. She's so squirmy that I even have a hard time keeping her still and preventing her from falling off the changing table! (Beth)

- Offer suggestions on how the baby-sitter can play with your baby. It will be very helpful if you point out his favorite books and toys.

- When your baby starts to develop separation anxiety, establish a ritual for when you leave. Some options are to say, "see you later alligator," or have the sitter hold your baby in front of the window so she can see you wave good-bye. This will help her predict the pattern that mommy leaves, someone else takes care of her, then mommy returns.

- It's not uncommon for new mothers to feel somewhat guilty the first few times they leave their baby with a baby-sitter. They worry that they shouldn't be putting their own personal pleasure before their baby's well-being. If you find yourself having these thoughts, remind yourself that you deserve to have some adult fun. When you give yourself permission to go out and enjoy yourself, you'll be more satisfied and relaxed with your whole life. That can only improve your ability to be a great mother. Feeling deprived or guilty won't.

- Tipping well is one of the best ways to keep good baby-sitters happy and eager to baby-sit for you. A dollar or two means a lot more to her than it does to you.

- It's your responsibility to pick up and drop off a baby-sitter. If she lives within walking distance, ask her parents whether they're comfortable with her walking to and from your home during daylight hours. If it's nighttime, you should always accompany her, even if she says she's willing to walk alone.

- Returning to a house that has toys everywhere can be a pain, but at least you know the baby-sitter played with the baby. If you want her to straighten up the toys she played with, let her know.

- No matter how often you use a baby-sitter and how comfortable you are with her abilities, occasionally come home much earlier than you said you would so you can see what's going on when you're not expected. You might want to give her a bigger tip or pay her for the full scheduled time.

- Trust your instincts. If you don't feel comfortable with a baby-sitter, stop using her no matter how good a friend or how close a family member she is.

Possible Indications of a Problem With a Baby-Sitter

YOUR BABY SEEMS AFRAID of that particular baby-sitter (more so than with other caregivers).

YOUR BABY SEEMS DIRTY.

FEWER THAN NORMAL DIAPERS WERE USED.

YOUR BABY IS UPSET or agitated when you get home.

THERE'S UNUSUAL TRASH (such as a pizza delivery box, cigarettes or items that didn't come from your house and weren't brought by the baby-sitter).

ITEMS OR SUPPLIES ARE MISSING (such as liquor, cigarettes, clothing or valuables).

YOUR CLOSET, DRAWERS, JEWELRY BOX, ETC. HAVE BEEN DISTURBED.

THE PHONE IS FREQUENTLY BUSY when you call to check in.

Finding and Using Child Care

Being responsible for your baby is one thing. Selecting someone else to care for her on a regular basis is another. You probably haven't been trained to write a job description or interview candidates, yet conducting a hiring process is exactly what you have to do to find someone to care for your baby when you're working or taking a well-deserved break from baby care.

The process of hiring a child care provider is often time-consuming, frustrating and stressful enough to make a grown woman cry. Unfortunately, the simplest approach isn't always the best approach. You don't want to run the risk of choosing a situation that makes the selection process easier now, but makes your life much more difficult later.

The best way to find the ideal type of child care for your particular situation is to go about it pro-actively. The most critical, but often forgotten step is to define what you want. Don't just consider the most obvious and popular choices. Instead, use the information in the next chapter to determine which child care option best suits your professional responsibilities, your personal lifestyle, your budget and the ways you want your baby's physical, emotional and social needs to be met, now and in the future.

Once that's done, you can conduct the search process. Again, don't just evaluate the situations that present themselves. Go out and network aggressively. Find options. Create opportunities. Then, as you learn out about different child care possibilities, evaluate how well they match what you want.

When you finally find a situation that works well for you, you'll probably be so relieved that you'll never want to think about child care again. Unfortunately, your responsibility doesn't end there. If you want your baby to continue to be in a loving, nurturing environment, you must continually evaluate the child care situation, handle existing and potential problems, and be aware of new options that might work better for both of you. Oh, and you have to pay for it and handle all the legalities, too.

CHAPTER THIRTY-FOUR

Deciding What Kind You Want

There are lots of different types of child care, including someone living in or coming to your house, child care at someone else's home and a child care center. For each of these options, there are many different versions. Unfortunately, I can't recommend a single best type of child care. I can only offer a sample of topics to consider when you're evaluating the choices. Only you can weigh the logistical and emotional factors and decide which type of child care best suits your needs and preferences.

As you review the following suggestions and your specific situation, make a list of all the criteria that define the ideal child care situation for you. Then prioritize it. This will help you rank your preferences for the type of child care you want. It will also help you make choices about what you are or aren't willing to give up if you can't find something that's exactly perfect.

- Money tends to be one of the first things parents think about when they're deciding what kind of child care they want or can afford. I suggest you think about it early on in the process, but set an upper limit on what you can spend instead of just defining a specific cost per hour or month. Another way to look at it is to determine the total amount of money you want to have left over after child care expenses are covered. This is especially important if you or your partner are making changes in your workstyle at the same time.

- There is probably a limit on what you can spend, but you should do an informal cost/benefit analysis on all your options. If a more expensive type of child care gives you the flexibility to earn more, for example, you might want to consider it.

I work with clients on an hourly basis. I found a day care provider I liked and who fit my budget, but she was rigid about her schedule. I worried about having to turn down extra time with clients because I had to pick Bobbie up from the child care provider at a specific time. I would also have to drop him off at a certain time, whether or not I was working that early. The only other child care provider I could find charged a few dollars more per hour, but was much more flexible about the schedule. I make so much more per hour than the child care provider charges that I decided it was worth it. I can earn a lot more and easily cover the additional hourly expense. Now Bobbie is only in child care during the hours I'm actually with a client. Not only am I more responsive to my clients' needs, but I'm a lot happier and less stressed when I pick up Bobbie, too. The total cost ends up being about the same. (Joannie)

I thought a nanny was way too expensive so I took Allie to a child care center. When I was about to turn down a promotion because I would have had to leave for work before the center opened, I knew I needed to rethink my options. I figured out that it was worth it to hire a nanny so I had more flexibility in my schedule and could take the better job. I'm paying more, but I'm also earning more. (Joanne)

- If you're considering using a nanny, remember that the cost includes the employment taxes you'll owe out of your pocket as well as the wages you'll pay her. See Chapter 37 for details.

- Money is certainly an important issue, but there may be creative ways to get what you want within your budget. Think about the ideal child care scenario without worrying about the cost, then figure out if you can make it fit your family's financial situation. For example, maybe you can share a nanny and the expenses with someone else. If you feel most comfortable with another mom taking care of your baby in her home, maybe you can trade part-time child care with a friend. Maybe you and your partner can coordinate your work schedules so the baby is with one of you more often and in child care for fewer hours.

- Another factor to consider is whether or not you want your baby to be with other babies or kids. Do you want your baby to have opportunities to learn social skills? Are you concerned about your baby being exposed to other kids' germs? If you have strong feelings about these two questions it will be very clear whether or not you want to use a child care center or an in-home child care environment (at the child care provider's home) with lots of other kids.

- If you're going to be using child care while you work, you need to consider your workstyle. Will you be working at home or away from home? Will you be working full-time or part-time? Will you be traveling? These criteria will help determine whether its better to have someone taking care of your baby in your home or to have your baby's child care at another location.

- Your family's schedule also dictates what type of child care will work for you. Is the schedule regular and predictable or flexible and changing? Do you and your partner work during regular business hours? What hours would you need child care?

- Also think about the total number of hours you need child care. Is it more or less than full-time? If it's part-time, how many hours total?

- When you're deciding what type of child care you want for your baby, you also have to consider what type of child care you want when she's a toddler or preschooler. You might not be able to answer this question yet, but it doesn't hurt to start thinking about it now. Ask yourself questions such as: Do you want her in a different type of child care setting when she's older? Do you prefer to keep her in the same setting until she's in school? Will you mind looking for another child care provider in a year or two if the provider only takes infants?

- As you think about child care for the future, be aware that an au pair, a caregiver visiting from a foreign country, usually hired through an au pair agency, can only stay in the country for a year. Some child care providers are only licensed for babies and toddlers, they don't care for preschoolers or older kids. Some nannies only want to care for babies and toddlers. Some child care centers can guarantee a place for your toddler or preschooler as long as he attended as an infant.

- If you're considering using an au pair or nanny, remember that her responsibilities don't include housework that's unrelated to the child care. You might want her to clean up after your baby, but don't expect her to clean up after you. You also shouldn't expect her to run the house while you're gone for business or personal travel. She might be happy to do it for a day or two, once in a while, but doing so on a regular basis isn't one of her responsibilities.

- Do you have back-up child care? If you rely on an individual child care provider, what will you do if she gets sick or takes a vacation? If you use a child care center, will you need child care on the holidays when they're closed?

- Also think about how involved you want to be in defining how your baby is cared for. If you want to set all the rules, you might want to have a child care provider who cares only for your baby. If you like having a well-structured, well-defined program, you might prefer a child care center.

- If you're considering hiring a nanny, be sure to consider whether you're comfortable handling all the legalities and financial responsibilities. (See Chapter 37 for a description of these responsibilities.) If you don't want to worry about taxes, insurance and right to work issues, don't hire someone as an employee.

- There are two options for a nanny. If you have a live-in nanny, you gain freedom, control and reliability, but you lose some privacy. If you have a live-out, it's important that she has dependable transportation and child care for her own kids. It's also helpful if you have a regular schedule for when you need her.

- Your personal feelings about the way you want your baby to be nurtured are also important. Do you want someone with a degree in early childhood development or a related subject caring for your baby? Do you want a loving mom taking care of him? Do you want him to be in a home environment or a school-type environment?

- Do you want to meet other moms with babies? If so, you might want to choose a child care scenario that provides you with social opportunities.

CHAPTER THIRTY-FIVE

Finding and Choosing Child Care

Finding Child Care Options

Finding child care is rarely a short, simple process. The only way to successfully accomplish the task is to talk to lots of different people, follow up every lead and try not to get discouraged. If you start to think there's nothing worse than looking for child care, you're wrong, there is—looking for child care again. The more carefully you handle the process the first time, the less likely you are to have to do it again in the near future.

- The process of finding child care can take months. Start looking for child care the minute you know you're going to need it, even if you're still pregnant at the time.

- The best way to find a child care provider who fits your needs is to tell everyone you know, and even some people you don't know, that you're looking for child care. Be sure to define exactly what kind of child care interests you. Ask people to contact you if they know of a child care provider or someone using a child care provider.

- Follow every lead you get. If a potential caregiver or child care center isn't able to care for your baby, ask for suggestions of other providers to contact. Follow the network from referral to referral until you find a situation that will work well for you and your baby.

- If you find a child care provider you like, but there isn't an opening for your baby, ask to be put on a waiting list. There's nothing wrong with

What to Try: To Find Child Care

Once you know what type of child care you want to use, you can use some or all of the following methods to find it.

CONTACT THE CHILD CARE AWARE PROGRAM of the National Association of Child Care Resource & Referral Agencies, 202-393-5501, for information on local referral agencies.

READ SITUATION WANTED ADS in various newspapers.

LOOK IN THE YELLOW PAGES under "Child Care," "Baby-sitting," "Schools," "Nanny Services," "Sitting Services," "Errands and Miscellaneous Services."

TALK TO FRIENDS.

TALK TO YOUR FRIENDS' CHILD CARE PROVIDERS.

CONTACT THE LOCAL GOVERNMENT AGENCY THAT LICENSES CHILD CARE PROVIDERS in your area.   If you have difficulty finding the licensing agency, contact the state, city, or county departments of social services, health, education, public welfare, human resources or family and children's services for assistance.

CHECK COMMUNITY BULLETIN BOARDS at community centers, grocery stores, local schools, places of worship, etc.

POST ADS ON COMMUNITY BULLETIN BOARDS.

RUN AN AD IN A NEWSPAPER. Specialty newspapers, such as community papers or newspapers that focus on family issues are often better than the major daily papers.

CONTACT YOUR AND YOUR BABY'S DOCTORS' OFFICES.

CONTACT JOB PLACEMENT OFFICES OF LOCAL COLLEGES and universities.

being on more than one waiting list, either. You never know when someone else's situation will change and an opening will become available.

• If you end up feeling as if your life will revolve around the schedules and needs of your caregivers, you won't be alone. Many new mothers find that child care plays a major role in their lives. Finding and keeping caring, competent child care providers takes time, effort and a lot of mental energy. Once you've established a good working relationship with the right one, though, you'll be able to relax and know that your baby is happy and healthy, even when you're not with her.

- Don't be surprised to find that your child care needs or the child care provider's availability change. You, like most moms, might have to look for child care again even if the first situation was great for a while. It won't be any more fun than last time, but hopefully it will be easier now that you know how to do it.

Evaluating Potential Child Care Providers

All child care providers aren't created equal. Sometimes there are well-defined, measurable differences. Other times you'll just have an intangible gut-feeling about their unique strengths and weaknesses. Both types of criteria are valid and important. Keep them in mind as you evaluate caregivers.

EVALUATING INDIVIDUAL CAREGIVERS

- Interview a lot of potential caregivers so you can compare and contrast them. Make sure to take notes so that you can remember your evaluation of each situation.

- The licensed versus unlicensed dilemma is a common one. You might feel more comfortable with a child care environment that is monitored for safety, but licensed child care for infants is very expensive and extremely hard to find in most areas. You like the idea of a mother who is doing child care so she can be home with her own kids, but how safe is the environment? Your best bet is to look into both options and make your decision based on how comfortable you are with each particular child care provider and her home environment.

- Licensing procedures, guidelines and requirements vary widely from state to state. Be aware that when a child care provider is licensed, it may or may not mean that her background was checked, that she has a limit on how many children she can care for, that she has guidelines for her schedule or the type of meals she provides, and that her information

---

Factors to Consider When Selecting a Child Care Provider

Most of the following questions apply to any individual caregiver, but some only apply to particular types of child care. Use what you need.

WHAT IS THE PROVIDER'S PHILOSOPHY on child care? (for example: babies should be on a strict schedule, babies shouldn't ever have to cry)

WHAT ARE THE PROVIDER'S TRAINING AND QUALIFICATIONS, in terms of education and infant safety?

IS SHE LICENSED? If so, is she licensed to care for babies and children or just babies. (Check with your local licensing agency for information on regulations regarding infant versus toddler care.)

WHAT WAS HER PREVIOUS EXPERIENCE? Who were her previous employers?

HOW LONG DID HER JOBS LAST with her previous employers? Why did those jobs end?

WHY DID SHE CHOSE TO WORK as a child care provider?

HOW LONG DOES SHE PLAN TO STAY in the child care business?

HOW MANY CHILDREN ARE UNDER HER CARE NOW?

WHAT IS THE MAXIMUM NUMBER OF CHILDREN that will be under her care at any one time?

---

is registered with the state. It probably does not mean that she has been trained or that her child care skills have been evaluated. Someone from the local licensing agency may visit her home to ensure that it continues to meet the safety requirements and that she doesn't have more kids than she is allowed, but these evaluations tend to occur on a very infrequent basis. If you want to know exactly what licensing involves in your state, contact your local licensing agency.

After following up on six levels or referrals, I finally found a licensed child care provider. The location wasn't terribly convenient, but I was so happy to find a space for an infant with someone who clearly followed all the rules and regulations, that I took it. The inconvenience of the drive wasn't as important as my piece of mind about my baby's safety. (Gloria)

HOW OLD ARE THE OTHER CHILDREN under her care?

IS THERE ANYONE ELSE IN THE HOME on a regular basis while your child is there?

IS THERE ANYONE ELSE WHO WILL BE INVOLVED IN CARING for your baby? (her teen-aged daughter, her mother, her friend, etc.)

WHAT'S THE DAILY SCHEDULE?

WHAT ACTIVITIES ARE DONE ON A REGULAR BASIS with the babies?

WHAT SUPPLIES, IF ANY, ARE PROVIDED? (food, formula, diapers, diaper wipes, etc.) What is the policy regarding cloth diapers?

ARE DAILY REPORTS PROVIDED? What topics do they address?

ARE THERE OPPORTUNITIES FOR PARENT INVOLVEMENT?

WHAT ARE THE PRICES and payment policies?

WHAT ARE THE POLICIES REGARDING PAYMENT for sick or vacation days?

WHAT ARE THE SCHEDULING POLICIES? (Can you change the days she cares for your baby, occasionally pick him up later than the scheduled time, etc.)

HOW WILL TAX MATTERS BE HANDLED?

I've had much better luck with unlicensed child care than with licensed child care. The licensed child care providers approached child care as a business. They want to have as many kids as they're legally allowed to handle, but some are willing to accept a few more on a part-time basis. They look at each child as being income, so they're willing to break the rules in order to make more money. One provider I talked to had as many as nine children in her house. Other licensed providers were absolutely rigid about schedules and rules. The unlicensed providers I found seemed to be doing child care because they love kids. They tend to know their personal limits and have fewer kids under their care. They're much more loving and flexible and much less expensive. For me, the choice is clear. (Jacque)

- Don't rely on a phone conversation to evaluate a potential caregiver. Meet with her at her home so you can get a first-hand perspective on her and her child care environment.

- Bring your baby with you when you meet with the caregiver. Observe the interaction between them, even if it's subtle. Consider whether the caregiver makes eye contact with the baby, smiles at her, makes an effort to make the baby comfortable with her before she tries to pick her up, etc.

- If a potential caregiver only questions matters that concern her (such as money, schedules, what you need to bring, etc.) without asking about your baby's temperament, favorite activities and familiarity with child care, find another child care provider. She's only considering your baby as a source of income, not as a person.

- Ask the child care provider for the name of at least one other parent who is using her now or has used her recently. If the caregiver won't provide references, I don't recommend using her.

Questions to Ask a Reference

IS THE CAREGIVER RELIABLE? Is she on time and available when she says she will be?

WHAT IS THE NATURE OF THE RELATIONSHIP between the caregiver and the children?

HOW CLEAN IS THE CHILD CARE FACILITY? How clean are the children under her care?

WHY DID YOU CHOOSE TO USE THIS CAREGIVER? If you don't use her anymore, why did you stop using her?

HOW LONG HAS YOUR CHILD BEEN UNDER THE CAREGIVER'S CARE?

WHAT DO YOU LIKE about the caregiver?

WHAT DON'T YOU LIKE about the caregiver?

WHAT PROBLEMS OCCURRED and how they were resolved?

WHAT HAVE OTHER PARENTS TOLD YOU about their experiences with the caregiver?

- Of course, the child care provider isn't going to refer you to someone who will give her a bad reference. You're more likely to get an objective source of information from a secondary reference, someone who is using or has used the caregiver, but whose name the caregiver didn't give you. So, ask the original reference person for the name of someone else who has used the caregiver.

- It's not enough to have the name of a reference. You have to call and talk to the reference.

- When you're close to hiring a particular licensed child care provider, it's a good idea to check her record by contacting your local child care licensing agency.

- Trust your instincts. If you're feeling uncomfortable about leaving your baby with someone, find another child care provider. It's not worth taking a risk. All you need to do is pick an excuse. Say that you found another child care provider whose location, schedule or program better suits your needs. You don't need to give any further explanation. Your baby's feelings are more important than the potential caregiver's.

- Obtain your caregiver's full name, home address, Social Security number, driver's license number and, if she'll be transporting your baby in her car, her license plate number. You can ask for it in the context of needed information for taxes and in case there's an accident or other problem and you need to track her down.

- There are companies that will conduct a background check on a potential child care provider. They use the type of information listed above to check references, previous employment, worker's compensation, and driving and criminal records. You can find these companies under the "Investigators" category in the yellow pages.

- If you're using an agency or placement service, screen the organization as carefully as you would screen the actual child care provider, especially if you're asked to give them a fee in advance. Carefully examine their policies regarding the nanny or au pair quitting, being fired or being laid-off.

One au pair came for two weeks, then left a note saying she had quit. It turns out that she had only signed on as an au pair to get to the United

States so she could be with her boyfriend. To add insult to injury, she left us with a huge long distance phone bill. I was really glad that the au pair agency helped us resolve the situation and find a new au pair who was committed to taking good care of Luke. (Alana)

- If you want to use a nanny, I suggest hiring her on a trial basis for a month or so. At the end of this period, meet with her to discuss how things are going. This is a good opportunity to suggest improvements and ask for her feedback if you plan to formally hire her. If you feel that she's not the appropriate nanny for you, you can merely tell her that you've chosen not to offer her a permanent position. This tends to be much easier than if you'd hired her and now have to formally fire her. If you want to hire a nanny through a nanny service, discuss their policies regarding this matter before you extend any type of offer.

Factors to Consider When Selecting a Child Care Center

Many of the same criteria that you would use to screen an individual caregiver, provided on page 236, can also be applied to the evaluation of individual teachers working in a child care center. In addition, consider the following criteria:

WHAT ARE THE EDUCATIONAL AND TRAINING REQUIREMENTS, in both early childhood education and infant safety, for teachers and teacher's aides?

HOW LONG HAVE THE TEACHERS AND AIDES IN THE INFANT ROOM been with the center?

WHAT'S THE INFANT/ADULT RATIO? (You probably want 4 or fewer infants per adult and no more than 6 children total per adult.)

HOW MANY CHILDREN ARE IN THE CHILD CARE FACILITY all together?

WHAT IS THE TEACHER AND TEACHER'S AIDE TURNOVER RATE?

ARE THERE ADULTS OTHER THAN THE PRIMARY CAREGIVER who will care for your baby? What are their qualifications?

EVALUATING CHILD CARE CENTERS

- Don't rely on brochures and conversations with directors of child care centers. Visit and meet with the actual caregivers to make sure they are really delivering what the organization promises.

- There can be big differences between locations and providers within child care center chains or franchises. Visit the actual center you'd use. Meet with the actual individuals who will be caring for your baby.

- Ask the child care center to provide references you can call. You can also just visit the center and talk to parents as they drop off or pick up their children. Be sure to ask these parents what they like and dislike about the center itself and the individual caregivers who work there.

EVALUATING CHILD CARE ENVIRONMENTS

- Unless you have someone taking care of your baby in your home, screening the individual child care provider isn't enough. You also have to evaluate the entire child care environment.

I once considered a day care center with a very good reputation. When I went over after work one day to visit the center and talk to the administrator, I ended up having to wait in line to get a parking space. Even though I felt very comfortable with all other aspects of the center, the parking problem was so significant that I decided to find another center. I just don't have an extra time in the morning or after work to wait for parking. (Claudia)

Factors to Consider When Evaluating a Child Care Environment

IS THE ENVIRONMENT BABY-FRIENDLY and baby-proof?

WHAT SAFETY MEASURES ARE IN PLACE? (fire extinguishers, working smoke alarms, first aid kit, accessible telephones etc.)

WHAT ARE THE EMERGENCY PROCEDURES if a child is hurt?

WHAT SECURITY MEASURES ARE IN PLACE? (badges for staff, locks on external doors, fencing, check-in and check-out procedures, etc.)

WHAT ARE THE SLEEPING ARRANGEMENTS? Will your baby have her own crib that isn't used by other babies? If cribs are shared, will the sheets be changed after every use?

HOW CLEAN ARE THE ROOMS in which your baby will play, sleep and eat? How clean is the facility in general?

HOW LARGE IS THE AREA in which the children play?

WILL YOUR BABY BE TAKEN OUTSIDE? If so, is the outside play area appropriate for a baby? Is the equipment clean and in good working order?

HOW CLOSE IS THE LOCATION to work and to your home?

IS THE ENVIRONMENT APPROPRIATE FOR WHEN YOUR BABY IS A TODDLER and a pre-schooler? (in case you want to continue to use this caregiver for the next few years)

IS THERE SUFFICIENT PARKING for parents dropping off and picking up children?

If you are considering an individual caregiver, the following factors also apply:

If she will be taking your baby in her car, **DOES SHE HAVE A SAFE, APPROPRIATELY INSTALLED CAR SEAT** or do you need to leave your car seat with her?

DOES SHE HAVE A CAR INSURANCE POLICY that covers personal injury?

If it's a home environment, **DOES THE CAREGIVER HAVE A RENTER'S OR HOMEOWNER'S INSURANCE POLICY** that covers medical expenses and liability?

CHAPTER THIRTY-SIX

Managing Child Care

Supervising a Care Giver in Your Home

The benefits of having a child care provider take care of your baby in your house can be enormous. You won't have to rush to get the baby ready to leave the house every morning. You'll know that your baby's environment is safe and stimulating. You'll also have lots of opportunities to interact with your baby and your caregiver. If you don't act like an employer, though, and fail to provide the appropriate input, suggestions, feedback, encouragement and recognition, you and your baby won't have the best possible experience. Following are some suggestions to help you avoid potential problems.

- Be explicit about your expectations and house rules. Typical problem areas include how much cooking or housework the nanny or au pair does, the number of hours worked and the work schedule. Unless you and your caregiver mutually agree that she'll cook for the family or do housecleaning, her role is to take care of the baby. Both of you should be expected to stick to the agreed-upon hours and responsibilities unless you both decide to change them.

- Other topics you might want to discuss when you first employ a nanny or au pair are:

  ❏ Taking the baby out of the house (for walks, to the park, on errands, to other people's houses, etc.)

❑ Straightening up after the baby

❑ Doing the baby's laundry

❑ Inviting visitors to your home

❑ TV usage

❑ Answering the phone

❑ Making phone calls (local and long distance)

- If your child care provider lives in your home, be sure to discuss how much you'd like her to participate as part of the family and how much she'll contribute, if any, for household expenses and personal expenses such as the telephone bill and groceries that are just for her. How much time she spends with the family when you and your partner are home is another issue that should be discussed before problems arise.

> *Lack of privacy was the hardest aspect of having an au pair. Her bedroom was right next to ours, my husband and I couldn't be alone together anywhere except in our bedroom, and I felt awkward about not inviting her along whenever we went out. In retrospect, the experience of having an au pair would have been much better if we had set and agreed to some ground rules in advance.* (Victoria)

- Typically, au pairs expect to be treated more like a part of the family than nannies do. You should invite your au pair to go out with you, include her in family events and make her feel at home as much as possible. However, you're not expected to include her in absolutely every activity. You and your au pair should discuss who will pay for her expenses when she's with the family. You don't have to pay, but it's a nice way to acknowledge a job well done.

- Remember that this person is working for you. While it's wonderful if you become friends, issues and concerns should be handled in a professional manner. The more you define the rules and expectations up front, the fewer the number of issues that will arise later.

- Come home early once in a while or drop in during the middle of the day so you can see what's going on when you're not expected at any moment.

  Once in a while I "forget" something on purpose. This gives me a good excuse to come home unexpectedly during the day. I feel better being able to make sure that Daniel is being well taken care of. It's worth having our nanny think I'm ditzy. (Sydney)

- Occasionally ask a friend to drop by unannounced. Have her report back to you on how things seem to be going in your absence.

- Set regular times, about every other month, to review how the situation is working out. This gives you both an opportunity to discuss your goals, expectations and feelings. Make sure you praise what your nanny or au pair is doing well. Don't just comment on the areas which need improvement. Also provide her with a chance to discuss her perspective.

- You know how difficult it is to care for a baby all day. Just because a nanny or au pair is getting paid for it doesn't mean that she needs praise or appreciation any less. Telling your caregiver how much you appreciate her and her efforts can make a big difference in her attitude and commitment. Positive feedback is a great motivator.

Monitoring Child Care Outside Your Home

Opportunities to find out what happens on a daily basis, get feedback about your baby, share your praise and make suggestions are usually short and hard to get when your caregiver is also caring for babies other than your own. Therefore, you have to be extremely pro-active in order to monitor child care outside your home.

- Schedule times to observe your baby in the child care setting. Even if the child care provider knows you're there, you can learn far more from what you see than from what someone tells you about what happens.

- It's a good idea to check what's going on even if you don't think there's a problem. Stop by unannounced. Come back early. You might be surprised by what you find.

One day I dropped off Javier at 10:00. The day care provider had told me that the kids only watched TV from 8:00 to 9:00 when parents were dropping off their kids. But when I got there, the TV was still on. It wasn't that big a deal, but it made me question whether she was doing everything else she had told me to expect. I also didn't want my baby just sitting in front of the TV. I brought the issue up with the provider, but she didn't think it was that big a deal. I did, so I found someone else. (Christina)

- If you have ideas, input or concerns for the caregiver, but one or both of you don't have time to talk at drop-off or pick-up time, send a note or make a call. Some contact is better than none.

- Set up times to meet with the caregiver to discuss how your baby is doing in the child care setting, how the caregiver is feeling about caring for your baby, how you and the caregiver are communicating, what's going well and what's not. Not only will this help you maintain the quality of your child care situation, but it gives you good practice for the parent/teacher conferences you'll have in the future.

- If the person who's there when you pick up your baby isn't the same person who takes care of your baby all day, make sure to talk with the primary caregiver on a regular basis.

- If your child care center gets a new teacher or aide, take the time to talk with her. Use the Factors to Consider When Selecting a Child Care Provider list on page 236 to determine whether or not you're comfortable with her caring for your baby. You don't have to formally interview her, but there's nothing wrong with chatting with her to make sure you agree with the child care center's hiring decision. If you don't, talk with the director about switching your child to a different room or making sure that other staff members are responsible for your baby.

Handling Child Care Problems

There are two types of child care problems. Each requires a different level of action. When you have concerns about the child care environment or the caregiver's relationship with you, it's worth trying to resolve the situation. Solving minor day-to-day problems is likely to be much easier than finding a new caregiver. If you identify a significant problem that relates directly to your baby's safety and happiness, however, quickly remove your baby from that situation. There's no point taking the chance that the caregiver will make the same mistake again. Don't wait until your baby has been traumatized to make a change. The guilt you'll experience in that situation will be far worse than the annoyance of finding a new provider.

DAY-TO-DAY PROBLEMS

- If you sense that your child care provider is unhappy or dissatisfied, ask her about it. It's better to get the issue out in the open than, in the worst case scenario, for her to become angry and take out her frustrations on your child, quit without notice, or act in passive-aggressive ways against you, such as misplacing things, showing up late or stealing. If you know what her issue or concern is, you can both decide whether to work it out or to end the relationship. Remember, even if you dislike confrontation or serious discussions, you're responsible for your baby. If the caregiver isn't happy, it could affect your baby's well-being.

- Occasionally, a nanny or au pair may forget that you're the woman of the house and the mother of the baby. She might get so involved that she starts doing things her own way or, worse, telling you how to do things. Acknowledge your caregiver when she has a valuable suggestion and, when she offers advice that you choose not to take, thank her and re-state how you would like things to be done. Don't let yourself be bullied.

- If an au pair or a nanny you hired through a service isn't working out, contact the agency regarding their policies and procedures for handling the situation. They probably have counseling support services that can help you resolve any problems. If not, they can assist you to replace the caregiver.

- If you have problems with a specific caregiver in a child care center that aren't resolved by speaking directly with the caregiver, talk with the director. Be specific about your concerns. Ask the director to describe exactly how she is going to handle the situation. Then observe the results. If the problem still isn't resolved, give the director more feedback, ask what's going on and discuss other options, including moving your baby into a different room, assigning other caregivers to his care or leaving the center.

SERIOUS CHILD CARE PROBLEMS

- If you suspect a major problem, such as abuse or neglect, immediately remove your baby from the situation. You might even want to talk to other parents whose children are in the provider's care. Report serious problems to your local licensing agency, the department of social services and/or the police.

- If you want to see exactly what's going on in your absence, there are companies which conduct hidden surveillance of child care providers. They can be found under the "Investigators" category in the yellow pages.

Possible Indications of a Serious Problem With Child Care in the Caregiver's Home or in a Center

YOUR BABY GETS EXTREMELY UPSET when she sees the provider. (i.e. she's upset about who she's with versus being upset that you're leaving)

YOUR BABY SEEMS DIRTY or unusually hungry.

YOUR BABY SEEMS TO BE HAVING AN UNUSUALLY LARGE NUMBER OF "ACCIDENTS" that leave a bruise or scrape.

YOUR BABY IS EXPERIENCING SIGNIFICANT DISTURBANCES in eating, sleeping and/or behavior patterns.

THERE IS A LOT OF TURNOVER in the group of kids. (i.e. the provider is continually losing old clients and gaining new ones)

THE HOME OR CENTER IS CONSISTENTLY DIRTY.

YOU FEEL UNEASY, but can't explain exactly why.

OTHER CHILDREN in the provider's care don't seem happy and playful.

THE PROVIDER GETS UPSET if you drop in unannounced.

Possible Indications of a Serious Problem With Child Care in Your Home

Besides the signals listed in the previous chart, there are some additional indications of problems when your caregiver works in your home:

YOUR BABY IS USUALLY UPSET or agitated when you get home.

THERE'S UNUSUAL TRASH (such as alcohol cans or bottles, cigarettes, or items that did not come from your house and weren't brought by the caregiver, possibly indicating that other people were in your home).

ITEMS OR SUPPLIES ARE MISSING (such as liquor, cigarettes, clothing or valuables).

YOUR CLOSET, DRAWERS, JEWELRY BOX, ETC. HAVE BEEN DISTURBED.

THE PHONE IS FREQUENTLY BUSY when you call to check in.

TOYS, BOOKS AND OTHER BABY ITEMS DON'T SEEM TO HAVE BEEN USED.

CHAPTER THIRTY-SEVEN

Tax, Legal and Insurance Aspects of Child Care

As if finding, selecting and managing child care providers aren't enough of a hassle, you also have to pay them and protect yourself from any financial risk. While the process of handling the taxes, legalities and insurance issues is frustrating and time-consuming, it's worth doing it right from the start. The process will only involve more paperwork, phone calls and potential penalties if you wait until there's a problem.

Tax Issues

- Two-income families or single parents can claim a credit for their child care expenses by completing Form 2441, Child and Dependent Care Expenses. The amount of your credit is based on your income and the amount you spend on child care, up to the allowable limit. The credit ranges between 20 percent and 30 percent of your child care expenses and is deducted directly from the total amount of tax you owe. Be sure to keep records of all your child care expenses.

FOR CHILD CARE OUTSIDE YOUR HOME

- If you use unlicensed child care in the caregiver's home, be sure to address tax issues. If you plan to report the amount you spend on child care as a tax credit, be sure to let your provider know. She may not have planned on reporting this income. Technically, she is supposed to claim this income, but many child care providers don't report cash they receive. If you report it, so should she. You will need her Social Security number in order to file your child care expenses as a tax credit.

- A licensed provider or child care center should provide you with an annual year-end statement of the amount you spent on child care. If they don't automatically give you one, ask for it.

FOR CHILD CARE IN YOUR HOME

The following information provides general guidelines on taxes. You should consult the IRS, state department of revenue, a tax preparation service, and/or an accountant for the specific rules that apply to your particular situation.

- If you have an au pair, you don't need to pay taxes on her income since she's working in the U.S. through a special cultural exchange visa.

- If you have a nanny who lives in or comes to your home, earns over $1,000 per year, is over 18 and isn't a member of your immediate family, she probably qualifies as a "household employee." In general, a household worker is an employee if you control what she does and how she does it, regardless of how many hours she works or whether you hired her through an agency. Therefore, if you give your caregiver specific instructions on what to do with your baby and how to care for him and she has a schedule for when she works for you, which you most likely do, then she's probably an employee. In contrast, a baby-sitter who's called on an as-needed basis, offers her baby-sitting services to other people, and can accept or turn down baby-sitting jobs when they're offered to her isn't a household employee. However, since there are many factors in determining whether or not your caregiver qualifies as an employee, it's a good idea to talk with a tax accountant about your particular situation.

- When you hire a child care provider other than an au pair to work in your home as a household employee, you must:

OBTAIN AN EMPLOYER IDENTIFICATION NUMBER, using Form SS-4, Application for Employer Identification Number.

HAVE YOUR EMPLOYEE COMPLETE A FORM W-4, Employee's Withholding Allowance Certificate. This informs you whether or not your employee wants you to withhold federal income taxes. If she does want you to withhold federal income taxes on her behalf, it also provides the information you need to determine the appropriate amount to withhold.

DEVELOP A RECORD-KEEPING SYSTEM to track wages paid and taxes withheld and paid.

OBTAIN, COMPLETE AND FILE THE NECESSARY STATE AND FEDERAL TAX FORMS.

- In general, the payroll taxes you owe for your household employee include:

FEDERAL EMPLOYMENT TAXES FOR SOCIAL SECURITY AND MEDICARE (FICA). The total tax due is approximately 15 percent of the cash wages. You as the employer must pay half of this tax out of your pocket, not her wages. The other half of the amount due can either be withheld, by you, from the employee's wages or you can pay the employee's tax for her, as some employers do as a type of benefit.

FEDERAL UNEMPLOYMENT TAX (FUTA): This tax is approximately .8% of FUTA wages, which are typically, the first $7,000 earned by the employee during the calendar year. This tax is not withheld from the employee's wages. You're responsible for paying this tax.

FEDERAL INCOME TAX: If requested by the employee (per her Form W-4), you withhold this tax from the employee's wages. The amount is based on a formula determined by the information on the Form W-4 that was filled out by the employee.

STATE TAXES: These may include unemployment as well as other state taxes. Contact your state department of revenue, a tax preparation service or an accountant for information on the laws in your state.

- Tax forms can be obtained from some libraries and post offices, the IRS (800-TAX-FORM), tax preparation services or an accountant.

- Once you report employment taxes to the IRS, the correct forms will be sent to you automatically.

- If you prefer to pay your federal employment taxes all at once, rather than on a quarterly basis (with Form 941), use Schedule H (Household Employment Taxes) of Form 1040. This form is included as part of your annual individual income tax return that is filed on April 15.

- If you use Schedule H, there are two ways you can avoid having to pay the federal employment-related taxes you owe all at once, when you file your annual tax return. One way is to have enough federal income tax withheld from your personal paycheck to cover the employment taxes you owe in addition to the personal taxes you owe. To do this, complete a Form W-4, Employee's Withholding Allowance Certificate, and give it to your employer. The other method is to make quarterly estimated tax payments, using Form 1040-ES, Estimated Tax for Individuals. Publication 505, *Tax Withholding and Estimated Tax*, provides additional information on these methods of paying your employment taxes.

- You must provide your employee with copies B, C, and 2 of Form W-2, Wage and Tax Statement, by January 31 of each year. Copy A must be sent to the Social Security Administration by the last day in February.

- The amount of taxes due is based on "cash wages." Cash wages are the payments you make with cash, checks or money orders. Money totaling up to $60 per month that you give your caregiver as reimbursement for her travel expenses for getting to and from your house aren't included. The value of food, lodging, or other non-cash items you give your employee isn't included, either. Money that you give her specifically to pay for these types of things is included.

- If you make an error and withhold too much from your employee's wages, repay the employee. If you withhold too little, withhold additional amounts from future payments to her.

- If you're the sole proprietor of a business and pay federal employment taxes for business employees or if you live on a farm, there may be different payment guidelines that apply to you. Contact the IRS, state revenue department, tax preparation service or an accountant for additional information.

- IRS Publication 503, *Child and Dependent Care Expenses*, is a good resource for additional information on child care taxes.

- Just in case you were wondering, if you're caught paying your child care provider "under the table," without paying any taxes, you'll probably have to pay a penalty and interest in addition to the amount of taxes that you owed. You may also have difficulty being appointed to a high-visibility public position in the future!

Legal Responsibilities

- The primary legal issue related to caregivers is the right to work in the United States.

- If you use a child care center, a caregiver who works out of her own home, or a nanny or au pair you hired through an agency, you don't have to worry about forms or procedures related to the right to work in the United States.

- If you hire a caregiver to work in your home without going through an agency, you must confirm that she is a citizen and, therefore, that she can legally work in the United States. To fulfill this obligation, get and keep a copy of her birth certificate, certificate of naturalization or certificate of citizenship. If she isn't a U.S. citizen, you must keep a copy of her Alien Resident Card (e.g. a green card).

- There are a multitude of forms and bureaucratic procedures to go through if you want to hire a caregiver who isn't an American citizen or doesn't have the appropriate work papers. Contact the Immigration and Naturalization Service (INS), your state's department of labor or an immigration lawyer for assistance.

Insurance Concerns

- Provide your caregiver with a medical release form that gives permission for emergency medical care to be provided for your baby in case you can't be reached. This release should indicate that your baby can be transported to a hospital or clinic and treated according to a doctor's recommendations. Be sure to formally sign and date the form. Also provide your complete insurance information.

- When you hire a nanny, whether or not she lives in your home, you should discuss insurance issues up front. They are often a key factor in whether or not you want to hire that nanny, how much salary you can pay her and whether she will accept your employment offer.

- Nanny agencies typically don't provide medical insurance, so it's up to you whether or not you want to pay for a nanny's medical insurance. Talk to your insurance agency about the pros and cons, costs and coverage options if you will be providing the coverage. Talk to her agency if you will be covering the expense of coverage she already has.

- In general, if a caregiver lives in your house and drives your car, you need to formally put her on your auto insurance policy in order for her to be covered in case of an accident. Check with your insurance agent for the specific rules that apply to your state and situation.

- In general, if your caregiver doesn't live in your house, you don't need to put her on your auto insurance policy for her to be covered when she's driving your car. Check with your insurance agent for the specific rules that apply to your state and situation.

- In general, if your baby will be riding in your caregiver's car, her insurance should cover personal injury to your child. Some states, however, don't require personal injury insurance, so you should check with your caregiver about her insurance coverage.

- Homeowner's and renter's insurance don't automatically cover your child in a child care provider's home. You should check with your child care provider to make sure she has homeowner's or renter's insurance that specifically covers her child care activities and provides a level of coverage that you're comfortable with. If your child is hurt in her home due to her negligence and her insurance doesn't cover it, your health insurance will have to cover it. In addition, you can sue her personally if she won't pay for the expenses.

- Contact your state's office of worker's compensation to determine whether you're required to carry Worker's Compensation insurance for a caregiver who is a working in your home. The regulations vary widely from state to state. In some places, this type of insurance isn't required for domestic workers. In others, there are specific rules determining whether a child care provider needs to be covered. If you're required to provide coverage or you choose to do so, contact an insurance company to purchase a policy.

- If your caregiver comes to your home, it's a good idea for you to have renter's or homeowner's insurance that will cover any injuries that she might sustain while she's there.

Our nanny slipped and broke her ankle when she was on an overseas trip with us. Not only was she without health insurance, but she tried to sue us even though I postponed my return home, missed weeks of work taking care of her and paid $1500 to cover out-of-pocket expenses.

Luckily, I had a special rider on my homeowner's policy that covered $4000 of her medical expenses. The insurance company even settled the legal case with her. Now I know to make sure that my nannies have health insurance, either their own or through my policy. I also get travel insurance to cover the costs of unexpected problems. (Nancy)

- Your homeowner's or renter's insurance covers the contents of your home and isn't affected by the identity of an individual who creates a claim. Therefore, anything broken by a caregiver in your home would be handled by your insurance company.

CHAPTER THIRTY-EIGHT

Choosing a Guardian

There's one more important legal decision you have to make about who will take care of your baby for you. You must designate a guardian to take care of her if something happens to you. This isn't a pleasant thing to think about, but luckily it isn't a responsibility that needs to be juggled along with everything else, or monitored like child care. You just need to do it once, do it soon and do it right. Oh, and while you're doing it, it's also a good time to think about your life insurance and other financial matters. You might as well get it all over with at once. You'll feel really good about having protected your baby's future when you're done.

- Choosing a guardian for your baby can be an emotional and difficult process, especially if you and your partner have differences of opinion. Nevertheless, grit your teeth and get through it. It will probably be better to make a compromise than not to make a choice at all.

- Write down the pros and cons of all the potential guardians to help you evaluate the choices. Consider factors such as their parenting style (or what you think it might be), their lifestyle, where they live, their financial situation, their relationship with the rest of your family and friends, their relationship with your baby and their track record of handling difficult situations. Many parents find that they feel the most comfortable selecting a guardian who could most likely give their child the life that they themselves would have liked to provide.

- Name only one person as the guardian. If you name a couple as guardians, there could be problems if they get divorced or separated in the future.

- Discuss your wishes with the person you're appointing as guardian. Make sure that person wants to be your baby's guardian.

- You might want to do more than just choose a guardian for your child. You can also designate certain people to be involved in decisions regarding different aspects of his life, such as education or religion.

  I wanted my younger brother to be the guardian of my child, but he was in college when Amanda was born. I didn't feel that this would be a good time in his life to be responsible for a baby. I decided to name someone else as the guardian if something happened to Sol and me before Amanda was five years old. I also indicated that under those circumstances my brother should be involved in all major decisions for her. (Peggy)

- Once you've chosen a guardian, you need to record your choice in a legal document. Your will should designate a guardian as well as deal with your finances and belongings.

  Deciding who should be Lily's guardian if something happened to Don and me wasn't that hard. Writing it down was. We had the papers sitting around for a long time before we finally went and got them notarized. That step just made it seem so real and final. Once we got over that emotional hurdle and put one copy in our safe deposit box and gave one copy to my sister, who would be the guardian, we felt very proud and responsible. We also got rid of all of our guilt for not having done it sooner. (Hope)

- The formal document which outlines your guardianship plans should either be prepared by a lawyer, or witnessed and notarized if you wrote it yourself. If you want to write your own will, there are a variety of books and computer software programs available to help you. Just make sure to select a resource which addresses guardianship in addition to estate planning. Also make sure that your state's laws recognize wills on pre-printed forms.

- Be aware that a judge views your designation of a guardian for your child as persuasive evidence, not the final decision. The court can make another choice if that's determined to be in the best interest of the child. However, if you describe the reasons why you want a certain person designated as your child's guardian, it could help the judge make the decision in your favor.

- If you have life insurance, now is a good time to check it. You might want to change the beneficiary and/or add to the value. If you don't already have life insurance, you might want to consider it.

- As your financial and family situations change, be sure to update your will. Protecting your baby's future, even if you won't be with him, is truly an act of motherly love.

Afterword

As your first year of motherhood comes to an end, I encourage you to take a look back at how far you've come. I hope that you've gotten so used to taking care of yourself while you care for your baby that it takes very little thought at all anymore. The habit should be so ingrained that you can hardly remember a time when you weren't able to do it so easily. It should also be so natural that there's little risk that you'll forget to do it while you're chasing after a busy, often exasperating, toddler.

Celebrate your success in enjoying, not just surviving, the challenges of the first year of motherhood. It is not an easy time for anyone, so don't discount what you've done. Then, once you've acknowledged your accomplishments, make sure to clearly define what's worked best for you so you can be sure to apply it in the future.

Remember that it isn't selfish to make decisions that allow you to achieve life balance and personal satisfaction. When you're happy and relaxed, you're more likely to have positive interactions with your child. You'll have more time for it, too. You're also going to provide him with a great role model for his own life. It's good for him to see you respect your own needs. It will help him learn to respect himself, as well as to respect you. After all, you wouldn't ever want to see your own child give up everything that's important to him for someone else would you?

Resource Guide

Following is a list of some manufacturers, organizations and associations you may need to contact during your first year of motherhood. Websites often provide helpful information that will answer your questions, but if you need more or can't find what you want, go the old-fashioned route and make some phone calls! If you're having difficulty finding a phone number for an organization that isn't listed here, call the toll-free directory at 800-555-1212 or ask a major baby retailer in your area for help.

If you have questions or need assistance, just pick up the phone and call someone. If the person you talk to can't help you, ask for a referral to someone who can. Sometimes it takes a few phone calls to get what you need, but in most cases, the answers to your questions are out there. You just need to find them.

Baby Equipment, Supplies and Toys

Consumer Product Safety Commission (recall info)
. . . . .800-638-2772, cpsc.gov

Juvenile Products Manufacturers Association (product safety brochures)
. . . . .856-231-8500, jpma.org

Toy Manufacturers of America (toy safety hotline)
. . . . .800-851-9955, toy-tma.org

Aprica 310-639-6387
Century 800-837-4044
Chicco . . . . .877-4-chicco, chiccousa.com
Child Craft . . . . .812-883-3111, childcraftind.com
Combi . . . . .800-752-6624, combi-intl.com
Cosco . . . . .800-544-1108, coscoinc.com
Emmaljunga . . . . .800-232-4411, emmaljunga.com
evenflo . . . . .800-233-5921, evenflo.com
First Years 800-225-0382
Fisher-Price . . . . .800-432-5437, fisher-price.com
Graco . . . . .800-345-4109, rubbermaid.com/graco

Kolcraft 800-453-7673
NoJo . . . . .877-824-9502, nojo.com
Peg Perego . . . . .219-482-8191, perego.com
Playskool 800-752-9755
today's kid 800-258-TOYS
Safety 1st (baby-proofing supplies) 800-739-7233, safety1st.com
Right Start Catalog . . . . .800-548-8531, rightstart.com
One Step Ahead Catalog . . . . .800-274--8440, one-step-ahead.com

Nursing/Pumping Breastmilk

Bosom Buddies 914-338-2038
La Leche League International . . . . .800-La Leche, lalecheleague.org
La Leche League International, recorded breast-feeding info
 ($1.99 per minute, average call five minutes) . . . 900-448-7475 ext. 55
Medela . . . . .800-435-8316, medela.com
Nursing Mother's Council . . . . .408-272-1448, fensende.com
International Lactation Consultant Association . . .703-560-7330, iblce.org
Visiting Nurse Association . . . . .800-426-2547, VNAA.org

Car Safety

American Academy of Pediatrics (car seat safety brochures)
 . . . . .800-433-9016, aap.org
DANA, Drivers Appeal for National Awareness
 (publicizes incompatible car safety systems and necessary
 modifications) . . . . .P.O. Box 1050 Germantown, MD 20875
The National Highway Traffic Safety Administration, Auto Safety Hotline
 (info on car seats and recalls) . . . . .800-424-9393, nhtsa.dot.gov
SafetyBeltSafe U.S.A. . . . . .800-745-SAFE, carseat.org

Safety at Home

Consumer Product Safety Commission (product recall info)
 . . . . .800-638-2772, cpsc.org
The Danny Foundation (crib safety checklist)
 . . . . .800-833-2669, dannyfoundation.org
Juvenile Products Manufacturers Association
 (write away for baby product safety brochures)
 . . .Two Greentree Centre, Suite 225, P.O. Box 955, Marlton, NJ 08053
National Child Abuse Hotline . . . . .800-4A Child

National Child Safety Council Child Watch (safety literature)
....800-222-1464
Perfectly Safe (catalog orders) 800-837-KIDS
Safety Zone (catalog orders) 800-999-3030

Child Care

Au Pair in America ....800-727-2437 x6188, aupairinamerica.com
National Association for Family Child Care 800-359-3817
National Association of Child Care Resource and Referral Agencies
....202-393-5501
IRS (for tax-related information) 800-829-1040
  (for publications and forms) 800-TAX-FORM
  (TDD for the hearing impaired) 800-829-4059

Miscellaneous Parenting Resources

Depression After Delivery 215-295-3994
Mothers at Home (newsletter and info for stay-at-home moms)
....800-783-4666, mah.org
National Association of Mothers Centers (community programs)
....800-645-3828
National Association of Postpartum Care Services
.........................P.O. Box 707, Pittsford, NY 14534
The National Parenting Center ....800-753-6667, tnpc.com
National Organization of Mothers of Twins Clubs 877-540-2200
Mom-o-Rama ....888-272-4671, spydergrrls.com
The Parenting Resource Center of the Web ....ParentsPlace.com
Resources for Infant Educarers 323-663-5330
Single Parent Resource Center 212-951-7030
Twin Services 510-524-0863

Suggested Reading
BOOKS RELATED TO LIFE WITH A BABY

The American Academy of Pediatrics, Caring for Your Baby and Young Child: Birth through Five, Steven P. Shelov, M.D. F.A.A.P. Editor-in-Chief

Baby Bargains: Secrets to saving 20% to 50% on baby furniture, equipment, clothes, toys, maternity wear and much, much more! by Denise & Alan Fields

Consumer Reports Guide to Baby Products
Differences in Development, by T. Berry Brazelton, M.D.

Dr. Mom: A Guide to Baby and Child Care by Marianne Neifert, M.D. with Anne Price and Nancy Dana

The First Twelve Months of Life: Your Baby's Growth Month by Month, by The Priceton Center for Infancy and Early Childhood

Infants & Mothers, by T. Berry Brazelton, M.D.

The RIE Manual: For Parent and Professionals, Edited by Magda Gerber (available from Resources for Infant Educarers, 323-663-5330)

What to Expect the First Year, by Arlene Eisenberg, Heidi E. Murkoff and Sandee E. Hathaway, B.S.N.

The Womanly Art of Breastfeeding and *The Breastfeeding Answer Book*, from La Leche League International (708-455-0125)

BOOKS ON PARENTING TODDLERS AND CHILDREN

The 7 Worst Things Parents Do, by John C. Friel, PhD. and Linda D. Friel, M.A.

Parenting with Love and Logic, Foster Cline, M.D. and Jim Fay

The Parent's Resource Almanac, by Beth DeFrancis

Touchpoints, by T. Berry Brazelton, M.D.

What To Expect the Toddler Years, by Arlene Eisenberg, Heidi E. Murkoff and Sandee E. Hathaway, B.S.N.

Win the Whining War and Other Skirmishes: A Family Peace Plan, by Cynthia Whitham, M.S.W.

Index

More from Perspective Publishing

Perspective Publishing is a small independent publishing company which helps parents with the problems you face every day: discipline, friendship problems, talking with your kids, balancing work and family, challenging and inspiring your kids.

The Guilt-Free Guide to Your New Life as a Mom: Practical ways to take care of yourself, your life & your baby – all the the same time
by Sheryl Gurrentz

Expectant and new moms need help with everything, and this easy-to-use practical book helps new mothers take care of themselves and everything else in their lives while taking care of their babies.

ISBN: 1-930085-01-X; paperback, 6"x9"; 250 pages; $14.95

Win the Whining War & Other Skirmishes: A family peace plan
by Cynthia Whitham, MSW

This easy-to-use guide helps parents increase cooperation and reduce conflict with children ages 2-12. Step-by-step, parents learn how to cut out all the annoying behavior (tantrums, teasing, dawdling, interrupting, complaining, etc.) that drives them crazy.

ISBN: 0-9622036-3-7, paperback. 6"x9"; 208 pages; $13.95

"The Answer is NO": Saying it and sticking to it
by Cynthia Whitham, MSW

Tackling twenty-six situations that plague parents of 2 to 12-year-olds, this book helps parents define their values, build good parenting habits, and set firm, fair limits. Bedtime, pets, makeup, music, TV, homework, and designer clothes are just a few of the problems covered.

ISBN: 0-9622036-4-5, paperback. 6"x9"; 224 pages; $13.95l

Survival Tips for Working Moms: 297 REAL Tips from REAL Moms
by Linda Goodman Pillsbury

Full of examples of how the tips actually work in real families, this is a light but no-nonsense practical resource thast can help every working mom. From chores to childcare, errands to exercise, this book makes life easier. Almost 100 cartoons make this a book you can't put down.

ISBN: 0-9622036-5-3, paperback. 6"x9"; 192 pages; $10.95

Good Friends Are Hard to Find: Help your child find, make and keep friends
by Fred Frankel, Ph.D.

Step-by-step, parents learn to help their 5 to 12-year-olds make friends and solve problems with other kids, including teasing, bullying and meanness. Based on UCLA's world renowned Children's Social Skills Program, this book teaches clinically tested techniques that really work.

ISBN: 0-9622036-7-X, paperback. 6"x9"; 242 pages; $13.95

Before She Gets Her Period:Talking to your daughter about menstruation
by Jessica B. Gillooly, Ph.D.

This friendly book has up-to-date information and uses real personal stories, exercises and activities to help parents talk with their daughters about menstruation — even if their daughters don't want to talk. It's the only book about menstruation written for parents.

ISBN: 0-9622036-9-6, paperback. 6"x9"; 166 pages; $13.95

Order now: 1-800-330-5851 or www.familyhelp.com (more on other side)

More from Perspective Publishing

The Summer Camp Handbook: Everything you need to find, choose and get ready for overnight camp—and skip the homesickness
by Christopher A. Thurber, PhD and Jon C. Malinowski. PhD
This practical book guides parents step-by-step through the entire process of choosing and sending children to overnight camp. It also includes extensive resource listings

ISBN: 1-930085-00-1; paperback. 6"x9"; 250 pages; $14.95

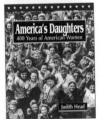

AMERICA'S DAUGHTERS: 400 Years of American Women
by Judith Head
This easy-to-read yet carefully researched history of American women from the 1600s to today is illustrated with 150 photos and period drawings, and gives children and adults both an overview of what life was like for women, and profiles of more than 50 individual women, both famous and not so well known.

ISBN: 0-9622036-8-8 Paperback. 8"x10"; 136 pages; $16.95

The Invasion of Planet Wampetter
by Samuel H. Pillsbury
illustrated by Matthew Angorn
Pudgy orange young wampetters Eloise and Gartrude Tub save their planet from becoming an intergalactic tourist trap in this non-violent and funny space adventure. As entertaining for grown-ups as for kids, it is a perfect family read aloud.

ISBN: 0-9622036-6-1, hardcover. 6"x9"; 144 pages; $15.00

9 TO 5 IS THE EASY PART

MomShirts
9 TO 5 IS THE EASY PART

100% cotton T-shirt
Sizes L, XL
$15.00

ORDER FORM

Qty	Title	Price/@	Total
____	America's Daughters	$16.95	_____
____	"The Answer is NO"	$13.95	_____
____	Before Period	$13.95	_____
____	Good Friends	$13.95	_____
____	Guilt-Free Guide	$14.95	_____
____	Planet Wampetter	$15.00	_____
____	Summer Camp	$14.95	_____

____	Survival Tips	$10.95	_____
____	Win the Whining War	$13.95	_____
____	MomShirt size L or XL	$15.00	_____
	Subtotal		_____
	Tax (CA residents 8%)		_____
	Shipping ($4 for 1st , $1 for @ add'l)		_____
	TOTAL ENCLOSED		_____

Name: _____

Organization: _____

Address: _____

City, State, Zip: _____

Phone: _____

Credit Card #: _____

Exp. Date: _____

Signature: _____

Send to: Perspective Publishing, Inc.
2528 Sleepy Hollow Dr. #A • Glendale, CA 91206
Or call: 1-800-330-5851
Or order on the internet: www.familyhelp.com

PERSPECTIVE PUBLISHING